ECONOMIC AND SOCIAL COMMISSION FOR ASIA AND THE PACIFIC

STATISTICAL PROFILES   No. 10

WOMEN IN CHINA

A COUNTRY PROFILE

UNITED NATIONS

New York, 1997

ST/ESCAP/1763

UNITED NATIONS PUBLICATION

Sales No. E.97.II.F.17

ISBN 92-1-119754-6

The profile has been prepared under project BK-X20-3-214 on improving statistics on women in the ESCAP region.

FOREWORD

The call for the development of statistics and indicators on the situation of women has, for some time, been voiced in various global and regional forums. It was first recommended by the World Plan of Action for the Implementation of the Objectives of the International Women's Year, adopted in 1975. The recommendations of the World Plan of Action were reaffirmed and elaborated in the Programme of Action for the Second Half of the United Nations Decade for Women: Equality, Development and Peace. On various occasions, the Commission, stressing the importance of social and human development, has recognized the need for improved statistics and indicators on women. It has noted that better indicators are required to monitor the situation of women and to assess the effectiveness of strategies and programmes designed to address priority gender issues.

The secretariat initiated the project on improving statistics on women in the ESCAP region in 1994. The project aims to support governments in their efforts to promote the full integration of women in development and improve their status in line with the Nairobi Forward-looking Strategies for the Advancement of Women adopted in 1985. The project has been implemented by the Economic and Social Commission for Asia and the Pacific (ESCAP) through its subprogramme on statistics, with funding assistance from the Government of the Netherlands.

As a major component of its activities, the project commissioned experts from 19 countries in the region to prepare country profiles on the situation of women and men in the family, at work, and in public life, by analysing available statistical data and information. The profiles are intended to highlight the areas where action is needed, and to raise the consciousness of readers about issues concerning women and men. The 19 countries are Bangladesh, China, India, Indonesia, the Islamic Republic of Iran, Japan, Nepal, Pakistan, the Philippines, the Republic of Korea, Sri Lanka and Thailand in Asia; and Cook Islands, Fiji, Papua New Guinea, Samoa, Solomon Islands, Tonga and Vanuatu in the Pacific.

The secretariat hosted two meetings each in Asia and in the Pacific as part of the project activities. In the first meeting, the experts discussed and agreed on the structure, format and contents of the country profiles, based on guidelines prepared by the secretariat through Ms C.N. Ericta, consultant. The second meeting was a workshop to review the draft profiles. Participants in the workshop included the country experts and invited representatives from national statistical offices of Brunei Darussalam, Hong Kong, the Lao People's Democratic Republic, Mongolia and Viet Nam in Asia; of Marshall Islands, Tuvalu, and Vanuatu in the Pacific; and representatives of United Nations organizations, specialized agencies and international organizations.

The original draft of the present profile, *Women in China,* was prepared by Ms Wu Jun, Director of Social and Scientific Statistics Department of the State Statistical Bureau. It was technically edited and modified by the ESCAP secretariat with the assistance of Mr S. Selvaratnam, consultant. The profiles express the views of the authors and not necessarily those of the secretariat.

I wish to express my sincere appreciation to the Government of the Netherlands for its generous financial support, which enabled the secretariat to implement the project.

Adrianus Mooy
Executive Secretary

CONTENTS

LIST OF TABLES

LIST OF TABLES *(continued)*

LIST OF FIGURES

LIST OF ANNEX TABLES

ix

PART I

DESCRIPTIVE ANALYSIS

INTRODUCTION

Traditionally, sons in China were considered to be advantageous for two economic reasons: support for their parents in old age, and the provision of labour for the farm and family business. Consequently, women were accorded a very low status within the family as well as in society. According to the feudalistic Confucian dogma of the past, women were regarded and treated as inferior creatures who had to obey their fathers until marriage, their husbands after marriage, and their sons after the death of their spouses. Women were also obliged to practise four virtues: morality, proper speech, modest manners, and diligent work. By and large, they were deprived of their rights to receive an education, take part in social activities, choose their marriage partners, and to remarry when widowed. Deprived of rights to own or inherit property, women were also economically dependent on men, and having no political rights they were completely excluded from social and political life.

With the founding of the People's Republic of China in 1949, a series of measures were taken to emancipate women and to establish equality between men and women as an important social norm. The Constitution of China stipulates that "women enjoy equal rights as men in all aspects such as politics, economy, culture, society and family life", which is the legal basis of equality between men and women. The important practical measures adopted to ensure gender equality include:

- The signing and ratification in 1980 of the Convention on the Elimination of All Forms of Discrimination Against Women. In order to make this Convention widely known, the government had translated it into Chinese languages and distributed printed copies of the translated versions among all sections of the population.

- The adoption in April 1985 of the Inheritance Law of the People's Republic of China which stipulated, *inter alia,* that

"men and women enjoy equal rights to heritage".

- The adoption in April 1986 of the General Rules on Civil Law of the People's Republic of China, which clearly states that women enjoy the same civil rights as men, and of the Compulsory Education Law of the People's Republic of China, which requires all children aged 6 years and over to attend school to receive compulsory education for a fixed period of years regardless of their sex, nationality and race.

- The adoption in April 1991 of the Civil Procedure Law of the People's Republic of China, providing detailed stipulations regarding women's rights and obligations in civil suits.

- The promulgation by the State Council, ministries and commissions of rules and regulations providing concrete stipulations in regard to the protection of women's rights to marriage, health care, employment, wages and salaries, and maternity leave.

- The promulgation in 1992 of the Law on the Protection of Women's Rights and Interests of the People's Republic of China, providing more firm and comprehensive stipulations in regard to the rights and interests of women in the field of politics, culture, education, labour, property, person, marriage and family. This Law constitutes an effective legal weapon for further enhancing the social status of women and guaranteeing their basic rights and interests. It also reflects China's commitment to observe the Convention on the Elimination of All Forms of Discrimination Against Women.

- The issuance in August 1995 of the Programme for Chinese Women's Development (1995-2000) which clearly states that the main goal for Chinese women's development is to improve the quality of their life in general and ensure that women enjoy all the rights they are entitled to by law. The Programme also lays down specific goals and related policy measures to achieve these goals.

While clearly delineating the rights and interests of women, the various laws also amplify the responsibilities of the relevant state organs in protecting women, and clarify the special status and role of the Women's Federation and other women's organizations in law suits, thus establishing a comprehensive mechanism for protecting women.

Since 1985, China has set up national organizations for the enhancement of women's status within the National People's Congress, the State Council and the Chinese People's Political Consultative Conference. These include the following:

- The State Council Working Committee on Women and Children, whose main functions are to coordinate and promote the work of the relevant government departments engaged in safeguarding the rights and interests of women and in implementing the National Programme of Action for Child Development in the 1990s; and to guide, urge and supervise the implementation of the Law on the Protection of Women's Rights and Interests.

- The Special Group for Women and Children of the Committee for Internal and Judicial Affairs under the National People's Congress, whose main functions are to propose, consider and process motions and bills on the protection of the lawful rights and interests of women and children as well as to urge and inspect the implementation of laws relating to women and children.

- The Commission for Women and Youth under the National Committee of the Chinese People's Political Consultative Conference, which supervises the implementation of the laws and regulations pertaining to women, youth and children, advises on further improvements and makes policy suggestions.

- The government has also given adequate support to women's organizations at various levels to implement appropriate programmes that would enable women to play a significant role in economic construction and community development. The All-China Women's Federation, founded in April 1949, represents and maintains the rights and interests of women and attempts to promote equality between men and women in the country. By the end of 1992, the Federation had set up more than 60,000 branches at or above the level of township and neighbourhood, 810,000 women's assemblies and nearly 130,000 women's committees at the grass-roots level.

With the necessary legislation and governmental machinery in place and dedicated women's organizations working in close collaboration with the bureaucracy, significant achievements have been made in promoting gender equality since 1949. Despite the great progress in the reduction of sexual inequality, male chauvinism and mistreatment of and discrimination against women are still evident in many areas. The 2000-year old traditional patriarchal feudal ideology which regarded males as superior to females still lingers in several parts of the country, particularly in the rural areas. The complete emancipation and development of women cannot be accomplished overnight. This makes it necessary to monitor constantly the implementation of various policies and programmes and the progress made in achieving stipulated goals and targets. There is also a need for continued advocacy and for appropriate development activities to ensure that women enjoy their rights.

The assessment of the current situation, identification of problem areas and adoption of corrective measures for enhancing the development of women require regular collection and detailed analysis of data on various issues concerning women. By and large, most of the data and information needed for these purposes are currently being collected, but there is a need for systematizing the process to ensure that available data are tabulated, analysed and presented in a comprehensive manner, not only to give a picture of the existing situation in regard to the status of women vis-à-vis men but also to pinpoint the gaps in the database. The present profile attempts to provide a model for the analysis and interpretation of available statistical data on a gender basis.

A. HIGHLIGHTS

The setting

1. In terms of physical size, China is the third largest country in the world, with a total land area of 9,571,300 square kilometres. Its topography is characterized by the five major landforms: mountains, plateaux, hills, plains and basins. Configuration and climate have greatly influenced the human settlement patterns and determined the regions suitable for development activities.

2. The supreme organ of state power is the National People's Congress, while the highest organ of administration is the State Council, headed by the Prime Minister. For the purposes of administration, China is divided into 22 provinces, 5 autonomous regions and 3 municipalities directly under the central government.

3. Notwithstanding the rapid economic growth since the establishment of the People's Republic in 1949, China is still a developing country, with a per capita gross national product (GNP) estimated at US$ 460 in 1993. Agriculture had been the backbone of the economy for a long time, but over the years rapid industrialization has changed the relative contribution of various sectors to gross domestic product (GDP).

4. There is a marked disparity in levels of development between major regions and in the standards of living between different groups of the population. There are about 70 million rural people living in poverty, mostly in the remote mountainous, hilly and plateau areas.

5. With a total population estimated at 1,158.7 million in 1993, China has the largest population in the world. A policy of controlling population growth has resulted in a decline in population growth rates in recent decades. Population distribution and density are extremely uneven, being heavily concentrated in areas near the coast. Only about 28 per cent of the country's population reside in urban settlements.

6. The Han Chinese constitute about 92 per cent of China's population, but the remaining 8 per cent is composed of over 55 officially recognized minority nationalities.

7. Since the founding of the People's Republic, China has made considerable progress in expanding educational and health facilities, and in improving literacy levels and the health status of the people.

Women's profile

1. Males have consistently outnumbered females in the total population at all census counts. According to the last census held in 1990, there were 106 males for every 100 females, or about 94 females for every 100 males in the country. The gender ratio varies across the 30 administrative divisions as well as between rural and urban areas.

2. A major factor contributing to the excess of males in the total population is the male-favoured sex ratio at birth, which in China has been substantially higher than the global average and has been increasing in recent years. The unusually high sex ratio at birth has something to do with the traditional belief that sons are superior to daughters.

3. Of the population aged 15 years and over, 70 per cent of females as against 66 per cent of males were reported to be married in 1990. The incidence of widowhood among females was considerably higher than among males.

4. Female mortality rates are lower than male rates at practically all ages. The overall maternal and child health status of China far exceeds that of most developing countries. The maternal mortality rate is now about 95 per 100,000 live births and the infant mortality rate is about 40-50 per 1,000 live births. However, there are significant regional variations in these two mortality rates, the rates for rural areas being about twice those in urban areas. The 1990 female life expectancy at birth of 70.4 years was 3.7 years longer than that of males.

5. Although China has made considerable strides in education, there are still significant disparities in enrolment and participation rates

as well as in the level of educational attainment between males and females. According to a 1992 sample survey, the enrolment ratio for children aged 7-11 years was 3.7 percentage points less than the corresponding rates for boys. About 70 per cent of children aged 7-11 years not enrolled in schools are girls. The percentage share of girls in total enrolments decreases with increasing levels of education.

6. The overall educational attainment and literacy levels of women are lower than those of men. In 1990, Chinese females aged 6 years and over had received on an average 1.6 years less education than their male counterparts. Women constitute about 70 per cent of the 182 million illiterate or semi-illiterate persons in China.

Women in family life

1. Historical changes have taken place in family relationships; the traditional family characterized by the authority of the husband and a patriarchal system has gradually been replaced by the modern family mode marked by equality, and a democratic and harmonious atmosphere.

2. Since 1953, the average Chinese family has become smaller owing to an increase in the number of nuclear families and a decline in the proportion of families with three or more generations. However, the three-generation family is still an important family type in China.

3. Great changes have also taken place in the people's concept about marriage and childbearing. The feudal marriage system characterized by arranged and forced marriages has virtually been abolished. Women have gained the right to make their own decision on marriage and are increasingly exercising that right to choose their own spouses.

4. A large majority of women marry late or past the legally stipulated minimum age of marriage; and the average age at first marriage has generally been increasing during the past two decades. The proportion of first marriages of women under 18 years of age had declined very significantly, from 48.3 per cent in 1955 to 6.2 per cent in 1980.

5. Chinese women now have the right to bear children and also the freedom to have no children. The total fertility rate (TFR), or number of children born to an average women, has declined from over five in 1970 to about two in the early 1990s, a fertility rate that approximates those of developed countries. Most of this decline occurred in the 1970s.

6. A one-child-per-couple policy is being strongly advocated by the government, but the policy has varied slightly from province to province. Some rural couples who have practical difficulties may be allowed to have a second child with approval, but with an interval of several years. Minority groups such as Tibetans and Mongolians may even have three children.

7. In order to meet the various needs of women, a network of maternal and child health (MCH) and family planning service stations have been set up nationwide. The network enables women to have access to safe, effective and convenient MCH and reproductive health services.

8. Most couples of childbearing age are using contraceptives and practising family planning of their own free will. Virtually every woman in China follows the same pattern of contraceptive use; she uses no birth control until the first child; then she uses an intra-uterine device (IUD) until the child (or children) passes the age of high mortality; and then, when she reaches the limit, she is sterilized.

9. People's attitudes towards divorce/separation have changed considerably; by and large divorce has come to be regarded as socially undesirable. Today a woman has as much right as a man to legally seek divorce.

Women in economic life

1. In traditional China, the involvement of women in directly remunerative economic activity was minimal as they were mostly engaged in household chores. The various legal and other measures adopted after the founding of the People's Republic had enabled an increasing number of women to engage in paid employment outside their homes.

2. According to census data, the number of employed females increased by 27.7 per cent between 1982 and 1990, the corresponding increase among males being 21.3 per cent. The proportionate share of females in the total number of employed persons increased from 43.7 per cent in 1982 to 45.0 per cent in 1990.

3. The larger increase in employed females has been due to the development of the market-oriented economy, which provided a favourable environment for women to work outside their homes, and to broadening employment opportunities in rural areas, which enabled an increasing number of rural women to participate in directly remunerative work.

4. Between 1982 and 1990, there was an increase in the number of females as well as males employed in various industrial or economic sectors. Nevertheless, the vast majority among both sexes were employed in the industrial sector termed "agriculture, forestry, animal husbandry and fishing". The proportion employed in this sector was significantly higher among females than among males.

5. During the eight-year period 1982-1990, the proportionate share among women in agriculture and allied occupations declined, while the proportion engaged in professional and technical occupations increased significantly.

6. Despite the increasing participation of women in the labour force, the occupational pattern of women's employment has changed very little over the years. Most women continue to be employed in the informal sector and are engaged in occupations characterized by low skills, low productivity, low wages and hence low status. The majority of females reported as "professional and technical" are engaged in such occupations as nursing and teaching, which require relatively low skills and carry less pay.

7. The principle of equal pay for equal work for men and women is in general practised in China, although some gaps in income still exist owing to current differences in educational and professional competence.

Women in public life

1. In the semi-feudal China of the past, women had no political rights and were virtually excluded from participating in political and public life. With the establishment of the People's Republic, Chinese women have come to enjoy the same political rights as men. Women of all ethnic groups and from all walks of life are today guaranteed their right to vote and stand for elections.

2. The number of women deputies in the National People's Congress had increased from 147 in 1954 to 626 in 1993, or from 12.0 per cent of the total membership to 21.0 per cent. During the same period, the proportionate share of women in the Standing Committee increased from 5.0 to 12.7 per cent. In the Central Committee of the Chinese Communist Party, the share of women in the total membership had increased steadily from 4.1 per cent in 1956 to 6.3 per cent in 1992.

3. At present, the Communist Party of China has over 7 million women members, accounting for 14 per cent of general membership. In one of the constituent parties, women account for 40 per cent of the members.

4. Women also play an important role in urban and municipal politics; in 1993, there were 308 women mayors and vice-mayors in the country's 517 cities. Chinese women also hold leadership positions in the party or government in 23 of the 30 administrative divisions and in 244 prefectures and 2,106 counties.

5. Despite the progress achieved, the percentage of women participating in political activities is still quite low, and the situation of unequal opportunities continues to exist. The substantial majority of political party members as well as party executives are males.

6. Studies also indicate that the vast majority of the women holding leadership positions are engaged in women's work or women's issues.

7. The number of women employed in government ministries and departments had increased from 10.04 million, or 31.2 per cent of the

total employees, in 1991 to 12.37 million, or 32.5 per cent, in 1994.

B. THE SETTING

1. Physical geography

China occupies a prominent geographic position in continental Asia, sharing its 20,000-kilometre land frontier with 14 countries: Democratic People's Republic of Korea, Mongolia, Russian Federation, Kazakhstan, Kyrgyztan, Tajikistan, Afghanistan, Pakistan, India, Nepal, Bhutan, Myanmar, Laos People's Democratic Republic, and Viet Nam. The Republic extends about 4,000 kilometres from north to south and 4,800 kilometres from east to west, encompassing a total land area of 9,571,300 square kilometres, or approximately 3.7 million square miles. In terms of size, China is the third largest country in the world.

The country's surface falls into three main steps or levels: the plateau of Tibet (Qinghai-Tibet plateau), with an average height of over 13,000 feet; an area of plateau and basins between 6,000 and 3,000 feet extending eastwards from the Tarim basin across Nei Mongol and the loess lands, then turning south to include the immensely fertile Sichuan basin and the Yunnan-Guizhou plateau; hills and plains lying below 1,500 feet, including the middle and lower Yangtze basin, the north China plain and the north-east plain. About 32 per cent of the land is mountainous, 26 per cent is plateau, 10 per cent is hill country, 20 per cent is occupied by basins and only 12 per cent is composed of plains.

China has over 5,000 rivers, some very long and some very short. The Huangha or Yellow River in the north is 4,845 kilometres long and has a drainage basin of 745,000 square kilometres. In central China, the Changjian is 5,800 kilometres long, with a massive drainage basin of 1.8 million square kilometres covering one fifth of the country. The shorter Xijiang or Sikiang River is the most important river in southern China. The rivers that water the plains bring rich harvests in some years, while in other years they may either cause flooding or dry up altogether, resulting in drought famines, a frequent occurrence until 1949.

Climate varies greatly with topography, latitude and distance from the sea. There are six broad temperature zones running from south to north: tropical; sub-tropical; warm temperate; temperate; cold temperate; and the Tibetan plateau area, which has its own characteristic regions. January is generally the coldest month and July the hottest. The summer monsoon brings plenty of rain to the coastal areas, particularly in the south and east. About 80 per cent of the precipitation falls between May and October, the wettest months being July and August.

Relief, configuration and climate have been very important in determining settlement areas and regions suitable for economic development. By and large, population and economic activity is concentrated in the limited area of the great plains, the valleys of the mountains and hills, and the river deltas. The geographical environment also poses considerable obstacles to modernization: the mountainous relief renders difficult and expensive the building of adequate transport links, which in turn causes difficulties in regard to shifting industries away from established centres in the east.

2. Government

The supreme organ of state power, in theory, is the National People's Congress (NPC), consisting of approximately 3,000 members indirectly elected from the lower-level People's Congress once in five years. NPC, which meets in a plenary session of two to three weeks once a year, usually in March and April, passes laws and treaties, nominates the executive and approves the Constitution. Between the annual plenary sessions, most powers of NPC are vested in a 200-member Standing Committee which drafts laws and handles NPC business.

The highest organ of state administration is the State Council, which in effect is the Cabinet, whose composition is decided by NPC acting on the recommendations of the Communist Party. The State Council is headed by a Prime Minister, whose term is more or less concurrent with the five-year term of NPC. The work of the State Council is presided over by an executive board of about 15 members composed of the Prime Minister, his deputies, state councillors and a secretary-general. Below the State Council come the various ministries and commissions, as well as a number of state-owned industrial enterprises.

For administrative purposes, the country is divided into 22 provinces, 5 autonomous regions and 3 municipalities, all of which are directly under the central government. Below the provincial level, administration is further subdivided into prefectures, counties, townships, and within cities into districts. The "communes", established during the Great Leap Forward of 1958 as the country's basic administrative unit, have been disbanded. At the end of 1991, there were 151 rural prefectures, 187 prefecture-level cities, 289 county-level cities and 1,894 counties.

3. The economy

China is a developing country with a per capita GDP estimated at US$ 460 in 1993. Traditionally, agriculture had constituted the foundation of the Chinese economy, but with rapid industrialization there have been remarkable changes in the relative contribution of various economic sectors to GDP. In 1993, the agricultural sector accounted for 21.2 per cent of GDP, as against 51.7 per cent by the manufacturing sector.

Chinese agriculture had made major advances since 1983 with the shift towards local autonomy and private initiative. Large-scale farm and water conservancy projects and promotion of the application of science and technology in agriculture were undertaken by local governments in 1990. In 1992, agricultural output grew by 3.7 per cent; the total grain production was estimated at 443 million tonnes, an increase of 1.7 per cent over that in 1991. The output of cash crops such as tea, sugar, tobacco, fruit and vegetables, as well as animal husbandry and aquatic products, improved in 1992 under the impetus of strong consumer demand (table 1). Nearly 59 per cent of the country's 1993 civilian labour force was engaged in the agriculture sector, including forestry, water conservancy and fishing.

The industrial sector has dominated the development efforts in recent decades. Indus-

Table 1. Per capita consumption of major consumer goods: 1978-1992

Consumer item	1978	1985	1990	1992
Food (kilograms)	195.5	251.7	238.0	235.9
Cooking oil (kilograms)	1.6	5.1	5.7	6.3
Pork (kilograms)	7.7	13.8	16.6	18.2
Cloth material (metres)	8.0	11.6	10.6	10.7
Coal (kilograms)	105.2	182.6	178.7	144.1

Source: State Statistical Bureau, *1994 Statistical Yearbook of China.*

trial production soared in the mid-1980s owing to strong consumer demand and increasing foreign involvement. The growth rate of the industrial sector, which averaged about 12 per cent in 1981-1985, had increased to 13.1 per cent by 1986-1990 and accelerated to an estimated 20.4 per cent in 1992. For the first time since 1982, the growth of heavy industries substantially outstripped that of light industries, as demand for investment goods surged. Heavy industry is largely concentrated in the north-eastern provinces, coastal areas and in major cities in south and central China. In 1992, the industrial sector, including mining, manufacturing, electricity, gas and water, employed 17.2 per cent of the civilian labour force (table 2).

In addition to the huge increases in industrial and agricultural production, the spectacular increases in rates of real economic growth experienced in recent years have also been fuelled by considerably high rates of fixed investment. China has been remarkably successful in attracting foreign investments; by the early 1990s, it was the largest recipient of foreign direct investment among the developing countries of the world. There are four special economic zones or areas within the country intended to attract foreign investment and technology. By the end of 1992, there were 84,371 registered enterprises with foreign capital in China, with a total capital of US$ 102.6 billion.

The rapid opening of the Chinese economy has also resulted in a dramatic growth in the external trade throughout the 1980s, and by 1988 the total trade was estimated at 100 billion United States dollars. There have been sharp increases in the export of manufactured goods,

**Table 2. Numerical and percentage distribution of the civilian labour force
by major economic sector: 1990 and 1992**

(Official estimates, thousand persons at 31 December)

Major sector	1990		1992	
	Number	Percentage	Number	Percentage
Industry[a]	96 970	17.1	102 192	17.2
Construction	24 610	4.3	27 016	4.7
Agriculture[b]	341 770	60.2	348 549	58.6
Transport, posts and telecommunications	14 690	2.6	15 727	2.7
Commerce[c]	29 370	5.2	23 118	5.6
Scientific research, culture education, public health etc.	21 670	3.8	22 689	3.8
Government agencies and people's organizations	10 790	1.9	11 480	1.9
Other	27 530	4.9	33 544	5.6
Total	567 400	100.0	594 315	100.0

Source: Europa Publishers Ltd., *The Far East and Australasia 1995*, 26th edition.

[a] Including mining, manufacturing, electricity, gas and water.
[b] Including forestry, water conservancy and fishing.
[c] Including catering trade, service trade, supply and marketing of materials and storage.

particularly clothing and textiles, with a concomitant decline in the relative significance of primary products, such as food and oil. Export growth was estimated at 16.5 per cent in 1992.

Although the national economy has been growing at a very fast pace, there has been a widening gap in the level of development and economic well-being between the more developed coastal areas and the less developed inland areas. The coastal areas, particularly the special economic zones, which have benefited from their accessibility, their links to overseas Chinese and their more developed infrastructure, had consistently shown higher rates of growth compared with the remote mountainous and arid areas as well as areas occupied by national minorities. For instance, estimated GNP per capita is 7,836 yuan in Shanghai but only 904 yuan in Guizhou Province. There is also a growing income differential among different social groups, with an increasing concentration of wealth among the newly emerged economic élite. There are at present 70 million impoverished rural people, most of whom live in areas that are generally characterized by their remoteness, lack of transportation, ecological imbalance, poor living conditions and slow economic development.

4. Demography

More people have lived under a single central government in China for the most part of that country's history than anywhere else in the world. The population of China, estimated at 412 million at the beginning of the Opium War in 1840, had increased to a little over 541 million by 1949, or by nearly 130 million in 109 years. The first national census held in 1953 reported a population of 582.6 million, which had increased to 691.2 million by the time of the second census taken in 1964 and further to 1,003.9 million by the third census conducted in 1982. According to the latest census held on 1 July 1990, the population of the country was 1,130.5 million, and official estimates give a population of 1,185.7 million at the end of 1993. These figures represent a more than doubling of the country's population during the four decades within the period 1953-1993, although the average annual growth rate had varied from one intercensal period to another (table 3 and figure 1).

In the global context, China is the most populous country and the only one to have attained the status of a demographic billionaire. It is also the largest developing country in the

**Table 3. Estimated and enumerated population of China, numerical and percentage increase,
and average annual population growth rate: 1840-1993**

Year	Population (millions)	Numerical increase (millions)	Percentage increase	Average annual growth rate (percentage)
1840[a]	412.0	–	–	–
1949[a]	541.7	129.7	31.5	0.25
1953[b]	582.6	40.9	7.6	1.82
1964[b]	691.2	108.6	18.6	1.55
July 1982[b]	1003.9	312.7	45.2	2.07
July 1990[b]	1130.5	126.6	12.6	1.48
December 1993[a]	1185.7	55.2	4.9	1.36

Sources: United Nations, *Case Studies in Population Policy: China,* Population Policy Paper No. 20 (New York, 1989); and State Statistical Bureau, *1994 Statistical Yearbook of China.*

[a] Estimates.
[b] Enumerated population.

world and bears the burden of having to support about 22 per cent of the world's population on about 7 per cent of the world's arable land. Since coming to power in 1949, the Government of the People's Republic of China has reacted to this demographic situation with a variety of policies ranging from pride in the size of the country's population during some periods to determined and strong efforts to control the population growth rates.

In 1980, a harsh one-child family policy was introduced with the objective of limiting the country's population to 1.2 billion by 2000 so as to ensure that population growth did not outpace socio-economic development, the availability of natural resources, and environmental protection efforts. Although the policy was relaxed in many areas based on the local situation, significant progress has been made in controlling population growth, promoting socio-economic development and improving the living standards of the people.

The growth rate of the population has been falling in recent decades owing to very significant reductions in fertility rates. The estimated TFR declined from around 6 children per woman in the 1950s and 1960s to as low as 2.4 in the late 1980s and has now reached almost replacement level, at about 2 children per woman (table 4). The crude death rate is also estimated to have declined, from about 25 per thousand population in the early years of the

Figure 1. Total population of China: 1949-1993

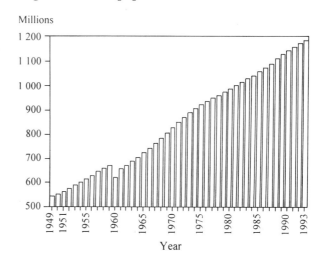

Source: "Population and development in China: facts and figures", *China Population Today,* vol. II, No. 3, 1994, Special Issue for the International Conference on Population and Development, Cairo, 1994.

People's Republic to a current low level of about 7 per thousand. The rate of growth of the population consequently declined from over 2.0 per cent per annum in the 1960s to about 1.1 per cent during the period 1990-1995. The current average annual growth rate for China is lower than the rate of 1.7 per cent for the ESCAP region as a whole.

The decline in fertility and mortality rates has also resulted in significant changes in the age structure of the population. For instance, the proportionate share of children in the total population decreased from 48.4 per cent in 1964

11

Table 4. Indicators of population change: 1950-1955 to 1990-1995

Indicators	1950-1955	1955-1960	1960-1965	1965-1970	1970-1975	1975-1980	1980-1985	1985-1990	1990-1995
Crude death rate[a]	25.0	20.6	17.1	10.9	6.3	6.7	6.6	6.7	7.2
Crude birth rate[a]	43.6	35.9	37.8	36.9	28.3	21.5	20.6	22.2	18.5
Total fertility rate[b]	6.11	5.48	5.61	5.94	4.76	3.26	2.50	2.41	1.95
Population growth rate[c]	1.87	1.53	2.07	2.61	2.21	1.48	1.38	1.53	1.11

Source: United Nations, *World Population Prospects: The 1994 Revision.*

[a] Per thousand population.
[b] Number of children per woman.
[c] Percentage.

to 33.6 per cent in 1982 and further to 27.7 per cent in 1990, while the proportion of the elderly (aged 60 years and over) increased from 6.8 to 8.6 per cent between 1964 and 1990. Consequently, the share of persons in the working ages, 15-59 years, recorded an increase from 44.8 to 63.7 per cent during the same period (annex table B.2 and figure 2). The median age of the population increased from 23 years in 1982 to 25 years in 1990; this means that in 1990 exactly 50 per cent of the population were below 25 years of age and the other half aged 25 years and over. In 1990, women of childbearing ages constituted 27.1 per cent of the total population.

On account of the vastness of the country and the great disparity in natural and socio-economic conditions in the different regions, there is a striking imbalance in the distribution of population across China. By and large, the population is heavily concentrated in the plain and riverine lands of the south-eastern part of the country, while most of the north-western part is, by comparison, thinly populated. In 1990, the south-eastern part, which accounts for only 36.5 per cent of the territory of China, contained nearly 95 per cent of the population, while the north-eastern half, spread over about 64 per cent of the total area, was inhabited by 5 per cent of the people. Such uneven distribution

Figure 2. Population pyramids for China: 1982 and 1990

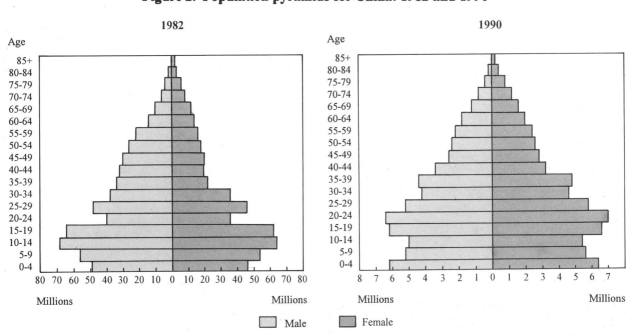

Source: Peng Peiyun, "The population of China: problems and strategy", *China Population Today*, vol. 9, No. 4, 1992.

has led to very high population density in the richest areas for settlement, such as the Changjiang Delta or the Red Basin of Sichuan. Indeed, 90 per cent of the country's people live in a little more than 15 per cent of the total land area.

The population of China remains predominantly rural, although the proportion living in areas designated as urban has been rising steadily since the late 1970s owing to increasing population mobility and urbanization. A readjustment of the criteria for building towns in 1984 also resulted in large numbers of newly built towns and the rise in the proportion of the urban population thereafter. Census data indicate that the relative share of the urban population in total population had doubled in 37 years, increasing from 13.3 per cent in 1953 to 26.7 per cent in 1990 (annex table B.3). In 1992, the urban population was estimated to be 27.6 per cent of the total population. Nevertheless, the population residing in cities and towns is relatively small compared with a large number of other countries in the region.

Table 5. Distribution of the 1992 estimated population by administrative division and population density

Administrative division	Area (thousand sq km)	Population at December 1992	
		Total (thousands)	Density (per sq km)
Provinces			
Sichuan (Szechwan)	567	109 980	194
Henan (Honan)	167	88 610	531
Shandong (Shantung)	153	86 100	563
Jiangsu (Kiangsu)	103	69 110	671
Guangdong (Kwangtung)	178	65 250	367
Hebei (Hopei)	188	62 750	334
Hunan (Hunan)	210	62 670	298
Anhui (Anhwei)	139	58 340	420
Hubei (Hupeh)	186	55 800	300
Zhejiang (Chekiang)	102	42 360	415
Liaoning (Liaoning)	146	40 160	275
Jiangxi (Kiangsi)	169	39 130	232
Yunnan (Yunnan)	394	38 320	97
Heilongjiang (Heilungkiang)	469	36 080	77
Shaanxi (Shensi)	206	34 050	165
Guizhou (Kweichow)	176	33 610	191
Fujian (Fukien)	121	31 160	258
Shanxi (Shansi)	156	29 790	191
Jilin (Kirin)	187	25 320	135
Gansu (Kansu)	454	23 140	51
Hainan[a]	34	6 860	202
Qinghai (Tsinghai)	721	4 610	6
Autonomous regions			
Guangxi Zhuang (Kwangsi Chuang)	236	43 800	186
Nei Mongol (Inner Mongolia)	1 183	22 070	19
Xinjiang Uygur (Sinkiang Uighur)	1 600	15 810	10
Ningxia Hui (Ninghsia Hui)	66	4 870	74
Tibet (Xizang)	1 228	2 280	2
Municipalities			
Shanghai (Shanghai)	6	13 450	2 242
Beijing (Peking)	17	11 020	648
Tianjin (Tientsin)	11	9 200	836
Total	9 571	1 171 710	122

Source: Europa Publishers Ltd., *The Far East and Australasia 1995,* 26th edition.

[a] Hainan Island, formerly part of Guangdong Province, became a separate province in 1988.

The slow rate of urbanization is due partly to the vigorous efforts to develop a diversified economy and small-scale industries in rural areas, and partly to the government policy of controlling the movement of rural population to urban centres.

5. Ethnicity

Although the Chinese people are relatively homogenous, China comprises diverse ethnic groups and languages. The Han Chinese group has been dominant in the country for centuries, and at the 1990 census constituted nearly 92 per cent of the total population. The Han Chinese inhabit China proper and the three north-eastern provinces of Heilongjiang, Jilin and Liaoning (collectively referred to as Manchuria), where Chinese migrants have been settled for many decades.

Approximately 91 million persons, or about 8 per cent of the population, belong to one of over 55 officially recognized non-Han groups collectively called minority nationalities. These minority population groups are mainly concentrated in peripheral areas and inhabit their autonomous regions or a regular Han province. According to the 1990 census, 18 of these minority nationalities number more than one million each. In recent decades, the minority groups as a whole have been growing faster than the majority Han Chinese because of a fall in death rates resulting from the provision of improved health services for the minority nationalities, while their fertility rate has remained high. In fact, several minority groups have been granted exemption from the one-child policy; the Tibetans and Mongol nomads, for example, are usually "allowed" three children. Owing to the higher growth rate, the proportion of minorities to the total population has also gradually increased, from about 5.8 per cent in 1964 to 6.7 per cent in 1982 and further to about 8 per cent in 1990.

China is a land of diverse languages belonging to several of the world's major linguistic families. The Han speak a number of related Sino-Tibetan languages that are collectively known as Chinese, of which Mandarin is the major form; other forms are Wu, Hsiang, Kan, Min, Hakka and Yueh. The various forms are mutually unintelligible when spoken but use a common ideographic writing system. Languages of other branches of the family, particularly the Tai and Tibeto-Burman branches, are spoken widely.

The minority nationalities speak languages of various branches (Turkic, Mongolian, Korean and Tungusie) of the Great Altaic family. The languages of the minorities are also unintelligible both to each other and to Chinese. Much less important are languages of the Austroasiatic and Indo-European families.

Linguistic differences between the seven main Chinese dialects as well as between Chinese and minority languages make bilingualism common and almost mandatory. In order to establish better linguistic communications, Mandarin has been adopted as the national language, and attempts are being made to simplify the written language by reducing the number of strokes in individual characters, and to promote literacy campaigns.

6. Social infrastructure

(a) Education

Under the semi-feudal and semi-colonial system of the past, China was educationally backward. At the time of the establishment of the People's Republic in 1949, about 80 per cent of the people were illiterate, only 20 per cent of children in the primary school age were enrolled in schools, and only one in every 18 persons participated in primary, secondary or higher education. By and large, women had no right to education at all. Most of the institutions of higher learning and technical education were then concentrated in the large and medium cities of the coastal provinces, while middle- and primary-level schools were mostly located in the county towns. Few villages had any schools and the situation was even worse in the remote parts and in areas inhabited by ethnic minorities.

Since the establishment of the People's Republic, education has been one of the strategic priorities in China's drive for modernization. However, education has had its ups and downs in the process of successive reforms.

The publication in May 1985 of the "Decision to Restructure the Education System" marked the most significant reform in Chinese education since 1949. It called for the provision of nine years of basic education for all school-age children and the devolution of responsibility for primary education to the local authorities; the development of vocational and technical education at the secondary and post-secondary stages; the restructuring of institutions of higher education by reforming the enrolment planning methods and job assignment system and by increasing their decision-making power and institutional autonomy; and improving educational management at all levels by strengthening the leadership at local levels.

As a result of the various policies adopted and endeavours made, tremendous changes have taken place and great progress has been achieved in the field of education. Compared with most developing countries, China has been remarkably successful not only in establishing a comprehensive system of education but also in providing almost universal primary education in rural areas and junior secondary education in urban areas. In 1993, there were 1.435 million schools, 10.979 million full-time teachers and an enrolment of 262.350 million students at all

levels of education. Today, more than 95 per cent of children aged 6-11 years are enrolled in primary schools (table 6), while more than 60 per cent at ages 12-15 years attend junior secondary schools. Nearly 75 per cent of children who complete primary-level education continue to the lower secondary schools, and 76 per cent of the counties have achieved universal compulsory education (junior secondary). In 1990, the literacy rate of the adult population aged 15 years and over was 78 per cent, compared with about 20 per cent in the late 1940s.

The impressive aggregate data cited above, however, conceal the considerable disparities in enrolment and participation rates between the economically advanced and underdeveloped regions, between urban and rural areas, between males and females, and between the majority Han population and the various minority nationalities. For example, while the goal of nine-year compulsory education has already been achieved in most large cities and coastal areas, many poor and remote areas have not even reached six years of universal primary education. The major goals of educational development in China during the 1990s continue to be universalization of secondary education in towns, cities and the more economically developed

Table 6. Selected indicators of educational progress in China: 1952-1990

Year	Students of different levels as percentage of total students			Primary enrolment rate (%)	Percentage primary-school graduates entering junior middle schools
	University and college students	Secondary school students	Primary school pupils		
1952	0.4	5.8	93.9	49.2	96.0
1957	0.6	9.9	89.5	61.7	44.2
1965	0.5	10.9	88.6	84.7	82.5
1978	0.4	31.1	68.5	95.5	87.7
1979	0.5	29.0	70.5	94.0	82.8
1980	0.6	27.8	71.6	93.9	75.9
1985	0.9	27.3	71.8	96.0	68.4
1986	1.0	28.5	70.5	96.4	69.5
1987	1.1	29.3	69.6	97.2	69.1
1988	1.1	29.3	69.7	97.2	70.4
1989	1.2	28.7	70.2	97.4	71.5
1990	1.2	29.1	69.7	97.8	74.6

Source: ESCAP, Human Resources Development: Effectiveness of Programme Delivery at the Local Level in Countries of the ESCAP Region, Development Papers No. 16, 1994.

rural areas; and the enrolment of at least 35 per cent of children aged 3-6 years in pre-school classes.

(b) Health

Until 1949, the health services in China were inadequate and standards of sanitation and hygiene were very poor. There were only 3,670 medical institutions, including 2,600 public and private hospitals, in the country and most of them were ill-equipped and provided relatively poor-quality service. For every 1,000 persons, there were then only 0.15 hospital beds, 0.67 doctors, 0.93 medical technicians and 0.06 nurses. Most of the medical institutions and personnel were concentrated in the urban areas, and the vast majority of the rural people were denied access to proper medical facilities and health services. Further, periodic epidemics, together with a high level of infectious disease morbidity and malnutrition, earned pre-1949 China its reputation as the "sick man of Asia".

Since 1950, increasing importance was being attached by the central, provincial and local governments to the development of the health services and improvement of the health status of the people. Over the past four decades, major emphasis was placed on a number of policies and strategies in the evolution of the nation's health-care system. An overriding priority has been the principle of equity of access or easy accessibility of health services to all citizens throughout the country. This has resulted in the nationwide development of a basic health-care network at the village and urban ward levels, as well as the establishment of well-organized supervisory and referral services at the township, county or district and city or provincial level.

The government's health policies have consistently encouraged the development of primary health care at the grass-roots level, that is the village, township and county levels, and this has led to the movement of medical personnel to the countryside. The policies also placed emphasis on prevention and the various public health programmes have been successful in rapidly bringing under control various infectious and epidemic diseases that typified the morbidity patterns in the past. The government's health strategies also aimed at the preservation and development of the traditional system of medicine simultaneously with the adoption of the modern system. Today, both systems coexist at all levels of the health-care sector, with health-care providers using both systems, depending on preferences. Another important strategy was the decentralization or delegation by central authorities of responsibility for the organization and implementation of health-care delivery to the local levels of administration.

Consequent upon the adoption of pragmatic policies and strategies, China has been successful in creating a comprehensive network of health services covering all counties, townships and villages. Today, every county has a county general hospital, an epidemic prevention station and a maternal child health station. Each township has a small hospital (15 beds) which provides both preventive and curative services to the population. About 86 per cent of the villages have a health clinic and most of the remainder are covered under outreach programmes. The total number of health institutions in the country increased from a mere 3,670 in 1949 to 191,742 in 1994 (table 7).

Over the years, China's population has attained a health status comparable with that of middle-income countries. Epidemic and endemic diseases, such as plague, cholera, malaria, smallpox and schistosomiasis, which were uncontrolled in the first half of this country, have been reduced to very low levels or even eradicated. Other infectious diseases, such as common childhood respiratory and diarrhoeal illnesses and adult tuberculosis, while still important public health problems, have been greatly reduced. In 1993, the average life expectancy at birth was 69 years, compared with 35 years in the immediate post-1949 period and 62 years for low-income countries; the infant mortality rate was 30 per thousand live births, compared with 200 in the 1940s.

Despite the vast overall improvements in the health status of the Chinese people, progress has been uneven because of the large size of the population that is spread across a vast country with diverse geography and unequal

Table 7. Health institutions in China: 1949-1994

Year	Hospitals		Clinics	Sanitation and anti-epidemic stations	Maternity and child care centres	Others	All health institutions
	Total	At or above county level					
1949	2 600	2 600	769	–	9	292	3 670
1952	3 540	3 540	29 050	147	2 379	3 871	38 987
1957	4 179	4 179	102 262	1 626	4 599	10 288	122 954
1962	34 379	5 300	172 708	2 208	2 636	6 054	217 985
1965	42 711	5 445	170 430	2 499	2 795	5 831	224 266
1970	64 822	6 030	79 600	1 714	1 058	2 629	149 823
1975	62 425	7 757	80 739	2 912	2 025	3 632	151 733
1980	65 450	9 478	102 474	3 105	2 610	6 914	180 553
1985	59 614	11 497	126 604	3 410	2 724	8 514	200 866
1990	62 454	13 489	129 332	3 618	2 820	10 510	208 734
1994	67 857	14 762	105 984	3 611	2 857	11 433	191 742

Source: State Statistical Bureau, *1995 Statistical Yearbook of China.*

social and economic development. The morbidity and mortality situation in the remote and poor regions does not compare favourably with other areas. The levels of communicable diseases are much higher than the national average, infant mortality rates in these localities are over 100 per thousand live births, while maternal mortality is approximately five times the national average. Hospital provision in relation to population also shows marked differences between urban and rural areas. By and large, the health conditions in cities are very good, but the health status of perhaps 100-200 million Chinese living in rural and remote areas remains similar to that prevailing in typical developing countries.

(c) Water supply and sanitation

China has adopted a multi-faceted health strategy, relying not only on curative and preventive activities of health personnel but also on cleaning up the water supply and promoting sanitary disposal of wastes. In 1990, an estimated 75 per cent of the rural population had access to improved water supplies. These estimates include all piped water systems, deep and shallow well handpumps and open-mouthed lined wells, where the most distant household is located within 500 metres horizontally and 100 metres vertically of the source. It is, however, unlikely that all improved water supply systems deliver "safe" water which would comply with the Chinese National Sanitary Standards for Drinking Water.

The percentage of the rural population with access to improved water supplies varies across administrative divisions in the country. In 1990, among the provinces, this proportion was highest in Hebei (95.1 per cent) followed by Shandong (92.0 per cent) while it ranged between 80 and 90 per cent in 11 other provinces and was below 50 per cent in three others. Of the five autonomous regions in the country, the proportion of rural population with access to improved water supplies was lowest in Tibet (16.8 per cent) and highest in Ningxia Hui (58.3 per cent), while in all three municipalities this proportion was over 95 per cent (table 8).

It has also been estimated that in 1990, over 216 million rural people were without access to improved water supplies, and that the majority of this unserved rural population inhabited the remote, higher altitude and minority populated areas of the country, where water scarcity may become acute during prolonged dry season periods or very cold and prolonged winters. Under these conditions, household members, mostly women and children, often spend hours fetching water for domestic needs. In remote rural areas, the designing, construction and maintenance of improved water supply schemes are also constrained by the lack of adequately qualified staff.

Since 1978, the National Patriotic Health Campaign Committee (NPHCC) and the Ministry of Public Health have been engaged in the

Table 8. Percentage of rural population using improved water supply by administrative division: 1985, 1987 and 1990

Administrative division	1985	1987	1990
Provinces			
Sichuan	38.3	40.7	60.6
Henan	60.2	73.3	86.3
Shandong	37.6	71.9	92.0
Jiangsu	49.4	57.0	81.4
Guangdong	n.a.	n.a.	87.4
Hebei	74.6	81.4	95.1
Hunan	73.5	86.4	77.2
Anhui	64.6	69.9	83.8
Hubei	27.6	42.4	62.2
Zhejiang	53.3	67.8	86.3
Liaoning	82.1	83.0	85.9
Jiangxi	43.3	61.9	81.7
Yunnan	26.1	30.0	42.8
Heilongjiang	59.7	77.5	85.3
Shaanxi	36.8	25.5	69.0
Guizhou	22.1	25.5	32.1
Fujian	57.5	62.2	88.0
Shanxi	63.2	73.0	78.4
Jilin	57.1	72.5	82.6
Gansu	16.4	26.9	37.0
Hainan	n.a.	n.a.	83.8
Qinghai	44.2	44.7	54.8
Autonomous regions			
Guangxi	35.9	43.6	61.0
Nei Mongol	35.5	42.7	54.6
Xinjiang Uygur	30.3	43.9	56.5
Ningxia Hui	49.7	56.3	58.3
Tibet	n.a.	n.a.	16.8
Municipalities			
Shanghai	75.5	81.2	95.5
Beijing	85.9	90.4	97.1
Tianjin	73.4	98.0	98.0

Source: UNICEF, "An analysis of the situation of children and women in China" (draft), Beijing, August 1992.

n.a. = not available.

accelerated development of hygienic standards of excreta management and disposal systems. Efforts to date have focused on higher density urban and peri-urban centres in the eastern coastal provinces. The issue of latrine affordability has become critical only more recently when efforts came to be redirected towards increasing the number of households with direct access to a hygienic latrine. NPHCC is planning to undertake a survey in order to determine the rates of access to hygienic latrines in the rural areas of the country.

C. WOMEN'S PROFILE

1. Demographic characteristics

(a) Gender balance

In China, as in most developing countries, males have outnumbered females in the total population. According to the data from the four national population censuses held since 1953, the proportionate share of females in the total population varied only slightly between 48.2 and 48.7 per cent between 1953 and 1990. In 1990, females accounted for 48.5 per cent of the population; in other words, there were then 94.3 females per 100 males, or 106.0 males per 100 females (table 9).

The age-specific sex ratios also indicate that in 1990 males outnumbered females at all ages excepting at older ages, 64 years and above. Men also substantially exceeded women at younger ages 0-9 years and at ages 40-54 years; at these ages the sex ratio, or number of males per 100 females, was clearly above the range observed in respect of normal populations (table 10).

The gender balance also varies among the 30 administrative divisions as well as between rural and urban areas of the country. In 1990, there was an excess of males over females in all provinces, autonomous regions and municipalities, although the sex ratios varied from one region to another. Among the provinces, the number of males per 100 females ranged from a low of 103.4 and 103.6 in Shandong and Jiangsu respectively to a high of 108.9 in Hainan, and in 12 provinces this ratio was higher than the national average of 106.0. Among the autonomous regions, the number of females almost equalled the number of males in Tibet at the 1990 census, although at earlier censuses there was an excess of females over males. In the other four autonomous regions, males significantly outnumbered females at all censuses. In two municipalities, Shanghai and Tianjin, females accounted for a little over 49 per cent of the population in 1990, but in Shanghai females had outnumbered the males

Table 9. Numerical and percentage distribution of the enumerated population by sex, and sex ratio: censuses of 1953, 1964, 1982 and 1990

| Census year | Enumerated population (thousands) | | | | | | Sex ratio | |
| | Both sexes | | Male | | Female | | Males per 100 females | Females per 100 males |
	Number	Percent-age	Number	Percent-age	Number	Percent-age		
1953	582 600	100.0	301 790	51.8	280 810	48.2	107.4	93.0
1964	691 220	100.0	354 790	51.3	336 430	48.7	105.4	94.8
1982	1 003 910	100.0	515 280	51.3	488 630	48.7	105.4	94.8
1990	1 130 510	100.0	581 820	51.5	548 690	48.5	106.0	94.3

Source: State Statistical Bureau, *1994 Statistical Yearbook of China.*

Table 10. Sex ratio (males/100 females) by age group: 1953-1990

| Age group | Sex ratio (males/100 females) | | | |
	1953	1964	1982	1990
0-4	106.8	105.7	107.1	110.2
5-9	112.7	109.8	106.2	108.2
10-14	117.7	108.9	106.0	106.7
15-19	109.6	108.7	103.6	105.4
20-24	104.9	108.8	103.8	104.4
25-29	105.4	113.6	106.5	105.4
30-34	106.0	112.4	108.3	108.8
35-39	107.3	110.3	111.3	106.7
40-44	108.2	107.2	114.2	109.8
45-49	104.2	103.8	112.3	111.3
50-54	104.3	100.6	111.6	112.1
55-59	102.3	90.9	106.7	101.5
60-64	94.3	85.1	100.4	106.0
65-69	84.7	78.3	91.7	96.3
70-74	73.4	68.6	81.3	86.0
75+	53.8	53.6	62.6	66.0
All ages	107.4	105.4	105.4	106.0

Source: Based on data in annex table B.1.

at the previous censuses. In Beijing, the number of males per 100 females had increased substantially, from 102.4 in 1982 to 107.0 in 1990 (annex tables C.2 and C.3). By and large, the preponderance of males in the total population was more marked in the provinces and autonomous regions located in central and western China compared with those in eastern China.

In 1982, as well as in 1990, the predominance of males in the total population was more significant in urban than in rural areas, although there were slight variations in the gender ratios during this eight-year period. Between 1982 and 1990, the number of males per 100 females declined from 109.9 to 108.6 in the urban areas and increased from 104.3 to 105.1 in the rural areas (table 11). The higher masculinity ratio in urban areas may be due to a higher proportion of males in the rural-to-urban migration streams.

The overall excess of males in the total population has been attributed to a combination of several factors, such as the higher female than male mortality, the traditional practice of female infanticide, possible under-enumeration of females at the censuses, and a male-favoured ratio at birth.

Table 11. Proportion of females in total population and sex ratios for urban and rural areas: 1982 and 1990

Year	Urban areas			Rural areas		
	Percentage female	Males/100 females	Females/100 males	Percentage female	Males/100 females	Females/100 males
1982	47.6	109.9	91.0	48.9	104.3	95.8
1990	47.9	108.6	92.0	48.7	105.1	95.1

Source: Based on data in annex table C.1.

As noted in the introduction, women were regarded and treated as inferior to men in the semi-feudal Chinese society of the past. The birth of a girl was never as welcome as that of a boy and may even have been considered a tragedy in a poor family or in one with no male offspring. The traditional male preference had invariably resulted in females being neglected as regards their food and health and consequently being exposed to greater risks of disease and death than males. Although accurate nationwide data are not available, it has generally been accepted that in the past female mortality rates were higher than male rates and this contributed significantly to a relatively lower proportion of females in the total population.

A tradition of infanticide and abandonment of infants had existed in China, particularly among poor families, prior to the foundation of the People's Republic in 1949. In really desperate situations when infanticide was practised, it was again the girls who were mostly the victims. Infanticide was reported to be more prevalent in Anhui, Henan, Guangdong and Guangxi than in other provinces. The preferential treatment given to male children, and infanticide, especially of females, were important factors contributing to marked imbalances between the sexes, particularly at younger age groups. It has to be mentioned, however, that abandonment of children and infanticide have decreased considerably as a result of measures adopted by the government, which viewed these practices as harmful.

Various estimates also indicate that the gap between male and female mortality rates has been narrowing over time and that in recent years female mortality rates at practically all

ages have been significantly lower than the corresponding male rates. Consequently, female expectation of life at birth has outstripped male expectation. In view of these developments and of the considerable reduction in female infanticide, it would be reasonable to expect a substantial increase in the share of females in the total population and a fall in the ratio of males per 100 females. But data from the censuses given in tables 9 and 10 show that, contrary to this expectation, the masculinity ratio had increased slightly from 105.4 in 1964 to 106.0 in 1990 and the sex ratios for ages 0-4 and 5-9 had increased substantially between 1982 and 1990.

It is likely that the observed preponderance of males in the total population could be due partly to a relatively greater under-reporting of women and children in the censuses, a phenomenon noted in respect of a large number of developing countries throughout the world. In China, the under-reporting of older children (above 5 years) in a census or survey is, by and large, less serious than the under-reporting of younger ones. A recent study by Zheng and others showed that relative under-reporting of female children contributed to the high sex ratios at ages 0-3 in the 1987 One-per-Cent Population Sample Survey. In an evaluation of the accuracy of the 1982 census data, Caldwell and others also highlighted the possibility of some parents of an only daughter being reluctant to admit the daughter's existence to either the household registration system or the census in the hope that they would not be discouraged from having a son.

Perhaps an important factor responsible for the deficit of females in the total population is the male-favoured sex ratio at birth. Analysis of registered births in a wide variety of countries throughout the world shows that the number of male births exceeds that of female births annually, and that the sex ratio at birth, or number of male births per 100 female births, is normally between 103 and 107. But in China, this ratio has generally been higher than the globally observed norm and is above 110 in some provinces. This unusually high ratio has something to do with the traditional belief that sons are superior to daughters. For instance, a study in 1994 by Coale and Banister based on population enumerations and fertility surveys revealed that in China the sex ratio at birth in the 1930s and 1940s was higher than normal, perhaps owing to higher than normal female infant mortality resulting from "the persistence of the traditional practice of infanticide".

A 1993 study by Zheng and others showed that the reported sex ratio at birth during the 1960s and 1970s was very close to 106, or generally within the normal range in most years. This may have been due to a reduction in female infanticide and female infant abandonment following the measures adopted by the government to modify these harmful practices. However, the sex ratio at birth increased during the 1980s, reaching 108.5 in 1981 (based on the 1982 census data), 110.9 in 1986 (according to the 1987 One-per-Cent Population Sample Survey), and 111.0 in 1987 (based on the 1988 Two-per-Thousand Fertility and Birth Control Sampling Survey) (figure 3). A recent analysis by Gu and Roy based on the 1990 census data reported a sex ratio at birth in 1989 of 111.3 for the country as a whole, but the ratio varied across the administrative divisions from a high of 117.4 in Guangxi and 116.7 in Zhejiang to a low of 103.4 in Guizhou and 103.6 in Tibet (table 12).

The rise in the sex ratio at birth during the 1980s has been attributed by Zheng and others to three factors: under-reporting of female births; an increase in prenatal sex identification by ultrasound and other diagnostic methods for the illegal purpose of gender-specific birth control; and a very low-level incidence of female infanticide. These factors in turn are largely related to two major developments: the introduction in 1980 of an official policy of one child per couple, and a drastic decline in fertility rates in recent decades in a socio-cultural setting where the strong traditional preference for sons still persists. It has to be noted, however, that in response to the discrepancy between male and female birth rates, laws and provincial-level regulations ban gender-testing of foetuses. For instance, article 32 of the 1994 Maternal Health Care Law strictly prohibits the use of technology to identify the gender of a foetus except for the diagnosis of gender-related diseases.

In 1980, the government introduced the "one child per couple policy". Since then the national fertility policy in China has been to advocate one child per couple, to control the second birth, and definitely to prevent the third birth. In practice, implementation of this policy has differed between regions and ethnic groups. In urban areas, second births are more strictly discouraged, while in rural areas there is more relaxed implementation in accordance with local conditions. Almost all provinces have begun officially to allow rural couples whose first child is a girl to have a second child. If both the spouses are themselves single children of their parents, then that couple is permitted to have two children. Couples belonging to national minorities are also allowed to bear more children. With the approval of the central government, six provinces and some pioneer areas in other provinces have even begun to test the policy of universally allowing two children per couple with appropriate spacing.

Figure 3. Sex ratio at birth: 1970-1989

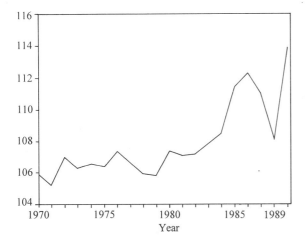

Year

Source: China Population Information and Research Centre, *China Population Today*, vol. 12, Nos. 3-4, 1995.

21

Table 12. Sex ratio at birth by administrative division and residence and total fertility rate by administrative division: 1989

Administrative division	Sex ratio at birth				Total fertility rate
	Total	City	Town	County	
Provinces					
Sichuan	112.1	108.9	106.0	112.8	1.758
Henan	116.2	113.0	113.9	116.6	2.897
Shandong	115.0	113.3	117.2	115.2	2.124
Jiangsu	113.8	112.0	107.3	114.5	1.939
Guangdong	111.3	114.0	120.5	109.1	2.512
Hebei	110.9	104.0	108.4	111.9	2.331
Hunan	110.1	105.6	111.1	110.5	2.397
Anhui	111.3	108.9	107.8	111.0	2.511
Hubei	109.5	108.8	115.0	109.4	2.496
Zheijiang	116.7	107.5	119.2	118.2	1.404
Liaoning	110.5	107.5	107.0	113.2	1.505
Jiangxi	110.4	112.8	112.1	109.9	2.460
Yunnan	107.3	103.9	105.3	107.6	2.588
Heilongjiang	107.3	105.5	106.4	108.6	1.713
Shaanxi	110.3	113.6	116.7	109.6	2.705
Guizhou	103.4	99.4	109.0	103.7	2.963
Fujian	109.9	109.4	124.0	108.9	2.362
Shanxi	110.1	111.5	109.3	109.9	2.461
Jilin	107.8	106.0	107.3	108.5	1.806
Gansu	108.4	106.6	112.6	108.5	2.340
Hainan	116.1	111.1	136.2	114.7	2.932
Qinghai	104.6	115.3	92.5	103.9	2.468
Autonomous regions					
Guangxi	117.4	113.2	110.4	118.1	2.727
Nei Mongol	108.5	105.2	105.3	110.1	1.967
Xinjiang Uygur	104.1	106.6	104.6	103.6	3.157
Ningxia Hui	109.7	111.8	110.0	109.4	2.614
Tibet	103.6	112.4	106.0	102.8	4.222
Municipalities					
Shanghai	104.1	103.9	104.0	104.7	1.344
Beijing	107.1	106.1	105.8	108.9	1.322
Tianjin	110.4	106.4	107.6	115.4	1.661
China	111.3	108.9	111.9	111.7	2.253

Source: Baochang Gu and Krishna Roy, "Sex ratio at birth in China, with reference to other areas in East Asia: what we know", *Asia-Pacific Population Journal*, vol. 10, No. 3, 1995.

As noted earlier, women's fertility in China, measured in terms of TFR, has declined considerably over the past four decades. More specifically, TFR is estimated to have declined by more than 50 per cent from 5.8 in 1970 to 2.2 in 1980 and fluctuated around 2.4 in most years during the 1980s. Estimates based on the 1990 census data indicate that in 1989, TFR had reached the near-replacement level of 2.25, although it varied widely across the 30 administrative divisions from a low of about 1.3 in Shanghai and Beijing municipalities to a high of 2.9 to 3.1 in Henan Guizhou, Hainan and Xinjiang, and to 4.2 in Tibet (table 12).

It has been argued that in a situation of high fertility, it is possible for couples to satisfy their preference for a male child through the number of children they plan to have, since some of them will in all probability be boys. But where fertility has declined dramatically to low levels, it will not be possible for couples to produce the number of children they desire owing either to the enforcement of a strict official population policy or to socio-economic constraints. In the specific context of China, where fertility had already declined to almost replacement level and national population policy demands more or less strict adherence to the one child per couple norm, parents will be more conscious of their sex preference for children and adopt a "quality for quantity" strategy, and even resort to illegal means to ensure that the child they are entitled to have is of the sex that they most desire.

Given this special scenario, couples will, by and large, deliberately refrain from reporting female births in order to avert penalties for having a high order birth or a birth forbidden by official policies. The 1993 study by Zheng and others showed that the under-reporting of female births accounted for about 43-75 per cent of the difference between the reported sex ratio at birth and the normal value of the true sex ratio at birth during the second half of the 1980s. Particularly in the rural areas, where the son preference is very strong, couples who have a high order male birth even consider it worthwhile to pay the penalty and report that birth so that the son can continue the family line.

In addition to the under-reporting of girls, an important cause of the imbalance in the sex ratio at birth is the misuse of ultrasound scanning machines. Zheng and others have argued that couples with the necessary resources will intentionally interfere with the fertility process to achieve their desire for a son by having a prenatal examination to identify the sex of the foetus and then a sex-selective induced abortion. Although more reliable information based on a large representative sample is not available, an analysis carried out by Beijing Medical University based on a small number of

aborted foetuses whose sex was identifiable (500 in rural and 1,226 in urban areas) indicated sex ratios of 94.6 and 96.8 respectively. Since these ratios are significantly lower than the normal foetal sex ratio, it has been suggested that some pregnant women had undergone prenatal sex identification and sex-selective abortion.

A detailed analysis of available data by birth parity indicates that the imbalance between reported male and female births has been occurring mostly at second and higher parity births. During the 1980s, the sex ratio at birth at parity 1 had remained more or less constant at the normal level, but the ratios in respect of higher order births have generally been not only higher but have also been increasing over the years. The analysis also indicates that the higher the order of birth, the higher has been the sex ratio at birth, and that the more recent the year, the higher has been this ratio. In 1989, the sex ratio at birth was 105.2 at parity 1 but reached 121.0 at parity 2, 124.3 at parity 3 and 131.7 at parity 4 (table 13).

The analysis of available data also indicates that an unusually higher sex ratio at birth occurs mainly among women who already have one or more children, but particularly among women having daughter(s) but no son, and that women with 6-8 years of education appear to have relatively higher sex ratios at birth. An analysis of the sex ratio by parity and sex composition of previous births in 29 administrative divisions also showed that the sex ratio at birth for women with previous

Table 13. Sex ratio (males/100 females) at birth: 1981-1989

Year	Order of birth					
	1	2	3	4	5	All births
1981	105.1	106.7	111.3	106.5	114.1	107.1
1982	106.6	105.2	109.4	112.9	109.9	107.2
1983	107.8	107.2	109.5	104.7	112.1	107.9
1984	102.5	113.3	113.0	115.3	127.3	108.5
1985	106.6	115.9	114.1	126.9	117.3	111.4
1986	105.4	116.9	123.1	125.3	123.5	112.3
1987	106.8	112.8	118.9	118.6	124.6	111.0
1988	101.5	114.5	117.1	123.1	108.7	108.1
1989	105.2	121.0	124.3	131.7	129.8	113.9

Source: Baochang Gu and Krishna Roy, "Sex ratio at birth in China, with reference to other areas in East Asia: what we know", *Asia-Pacific Population Journal*, vol. 10, No. 3, 1995.

births of all male children tended to be very low in the provinces.

Studies have also reported that female infant mortality increased during the 1980s. The increase in the reported female mortality at age 0 and the persistence of a higher reported female mortality at ages 1-4 are quite alarming, although female mortality is lower than male mortality at every age group above age 5 years.

The spectacular rise in the reported sex ratios at birth during the 1980s, especially during the latter half of this decade, is also reflected in the abnormally high sex ratio (number of males per 100 females) of persons in very young age groups. According to the 1990 census, the sex ratio of 110.2 for children aged 0-4 years was considerably higher than normal, that for 5-9 years of 108.2 was slightly above, and those for the 10-14 and 15-19 age groups were within the normal range (table 10).

(b) Age structure

As noted in the previous section, "The setting", there have been changes in the age composition of the population as a result of changes in fertility and mortality rates over time. The percentage distribution of the enumerated population by age groups and sex given in annex table B.2 shows that between 1982 and 1990 the proportion of children aged 0-14 years had declined significantly, by 5.4 percentage points for males and by 6.5 percentage points for females. Concomitantly, the proportion of persons in the working ages 15-59 years had increased by 3.6 percentage points for males and by 4.4 percentage points for females. In 1990, nearly two thirds of all males and females were concentrated in the working ages. In that year, the proportion of elderly persons aged 60 years and over was higher among females (9.8 per cent) compared with males (8.8 per cent).

The substantially high proportion of the population at ages 15-59 has several socio-economic and demographic implications. In the first instance, the number of males and females entering the labour market and seeking employ-

ment is bound to increase in the immediate future, placing a great burden on the economy for the creation of an adequate number of job opportunities. Second, a large proportion of women at ages 15-59 also means that the number of women in reproductive ages 15-49 years will increase over the years. This in turn means that there will be a substantial addition to the total population, even if fertility rates were to decline over the years.

As a result of the "baby boom" of the 1950s, there have been very significant increases in the number as well as the proportion of women in the reproductive ages 15-49 years. Estimates indicate that the number of women in this cohort increased by 23 per cent from 252.0 million in 1982 to 310.4 million in 1990, and further to 329.5 million in 1995 (table 14), and that the proportionate share of women aged 15-49 years among women of all ages increased from 50.9 per cent in 1982 to 55.7 per cent in 1990 (annex table B.2).

It is also evident from table 14 that the number of women in prime fertility ages 20-29 years has also been increasing numerically, from 83.7 million in 1982 to 116.3 million in 1990, and in relative terms from 33.2 to 37.4 per cent of all women aged 15-49 years during the same period. The number of women in prime fertility ages is estimated to have increased further to 123.7 million in 1992, thereafter declining gradually to 119.0 million in 1995. The number of women at peak fertility age, 23 years, had more than doubled between 1983 and 1986 (from 6.0 million to 13.4 million), thereafter declining to about 11.2 million in 1990. Their proportionate share in the total number of women aged 15-49 years also increased markedly, from 2.3 per cent in 1983 to 4.7 per cent in 1986, thereafter declining to 3.6 per cent in 1990.

(c) Marital status

Among the population aged 15 years and over, 70.0 per cent of females compared with 66.4 per cent of males were reported to be currently married at the time of the 1990 census. The proportion remaining single or unmarried was higher among males (29.0 per cent) than

Table 14. Numerical and percentage distribution of women aged 15-49 years by prime fertility and peak fertility ages: 1982-1995

Year	Women aged 15-49 years		Women in prime fertility age group 20-29		Women in peak fertility age 23 years	
	Number (millions)	Percentage	Number (millions)	Percentage	Number (millions)	Percentage
1982	252.0	100.0	83.68	33.2	6.88	2.7
1983	260.0	100.0	88.27	34.0	6.01	2.3
1984	268.5	100.0	90.85	33.8	6.18	2.3
1985	276.7	100.0	93.90	33.9	11.02	4.0
1986	285.5	100.0	96.70	33.9	13.39	4.7
1987	291.7	100.0	98.44	33.7	11.97	4.1
1988	298.9	100.0	102.10	34.2	12.18	4.1
1989	305.2	100.0	109.44	35.9	11.66	3.8
1990	310.4	100.0	116.32	37.4	11.17	3.6
1991	314.8	100.0	122.72	39.0	12.79	4.1
1992	318.9	100.0	123.72	38.8	13.25	4.2
1993	323.0	100.0	122.17	37.8	12.94	4.0
1994	326.8	100.0	121.17	37.1	12.63	3.9
1995	329.5	100.0	119.04	36.1	12.03	3.7

Source: China Population Information and Research Centre, *China Population Today*, vol. 12, Nos. 3-4, 1995.

among females (21.1 per cent). The 1990 census also revealed that the incidence of widowhood among females (8.5 per cent) was more than double the incidence of 3.8 per cent reported in respect of all males aged 15 years and over. The incidence of divorce/separation is very low in China, but the percentage divorced among males (0.8 per cent) was double that for females (table 15).

There were, however, significant changes in the marital status pattern between 1982 and 1990. During this eight-year period, there was a decline in the proportions unmarried and widowed, and an increase in the proportions married, among both males and females. The proportion unmarried declined by 3.7 percentage points for males and by 3.1 percentage points for females, while the proportions married increased by 4.5 percentage points for both males and females (table 16).

According to the 1990 census data, the pattern of marital status was, by and large, similar across the various administrative divisions, with the proportion married among females aged 15 years and over being higher than the corresponding proportions for males in all provinces, administrative regions and municipalities, except in Tibet, where a higher proportion among males

Table 15. Numerical and percentage distribution of persons aged 15 years and over by marital status and sex: 1990 census

Marital status	Both sexes		Male		Female	
	Number (thousands)	Percent-age	Number (thousands)	Percent-age	Number (thousands)	Percent-age
Unmarried	205 404.8	25.1	121 303.5	29.0	84 101.3	21.1
Married	557 373.1	68.2	278 265.6	66.4	279 107.5	70.0
Widowed	49 893.3	6.1	15 914.7	3.8	33 978.6	8.5
Divorced	4 837.6	0.6	3 473.0	0.8	1 364.6	0.4
All statuses	817 508.8	100.0	418 956.8	100.0	398 552.0	100.0

Source: State Statistical Bureau, *1994 Statistical Yearbook of China.*

Table 16. Percentage distribution of persons aged 15 years and over by marital status and sex: 1982 and 1990 censuses

Marital status	1982		1990	
	Male	Female	Male	Female
Unmarried	32.7	24.2	29.0	21.1
Married	61.9	65.5	66.4	70.0
Widowed	4.5	10.0	3.8	8.5
Divorced	0.9	0.3	0.8	0.4
All statuses	100.0	100.0	100.0	100.0

Sources: Major figures by 10 per cent sample tabulation on the 1982 population census; and State Statistical Bureau, *1994 Statistical Yearbook of China.*

than females were reported as married. Tibet is also the only region where the reported percentage married is considerably lower and the percentage unmarried considerably higher for both males and females compared with the respective national averages (table 17).

In 1990, there were 16 administrative divisions in which the proportion married among females was higher than the national average; in 16 provinces, the proportion of single females was higher than the national average. In all provinces, the incidence of widowhood was considerably higher among females than males; nearly one tenth of all females were reported to be widowed in Guangdong, Shanghai, Tibet, Gansu, Zheijiang, Fujian and Hainan (table 17).

Marital status rates also vary according to the level of educational attainment of persons aged 15 years and over. The 1990 census data showed that the proportion of women reported as married was over 70 per cent for those with primary education (74.0 per cent) and those who were illiterate or semi-illiterate (72.1 per cent), but was only 59.5 per cent for women with university degrees. In other words, the probability of marriage was generally greater for women with no education or some education compared with women having higher levels of educational attainment. Although no definite correlation could be established between the level of education and the probability of marriage for males, the 1990 census data showed that the proportion of men reported as married was highest for those with junior college degrees (74.2 per cent), followed by those with tech-

nical secondary education (69.7 per cent) and primary-level education (69.2 per cent).

Further, nearly 38 per cent of women and 35 per cent of men with university degrees were unmarried. The proportion remaining single was also over 30 per cent among women with junior middle, senior middle, technical secondary and junior college education. The incidence of widowhood for males and females was highest among those who were illiterate or semi-illiterate (table 18).

2. Health status

Since the founding of the People's Republic in 1949, the health of women and children has been accorded high national priority, and the government has systematically carried out maternal and child health (MCH) activities and developed the necessary institutions and manpower. The Maternal and Child Health Department in the Ministry of Public Health is the main technical department responsible for establishing policy for safeguarding the health of women and children. The departments responsible for public health at different levels of government have corresponding MCH agencies. By the end of 1992, there were 346 maternity and child care institutions and 2,841 MCH centres throughout the country, with a total number of 50,236 beds and 106,000 medical workers.

Over the years, considerable progress has been made in reducing morbidity and mortality and in improving nutrition among women and children. In the mid-1970s, the mortality rate

Table 17. Percentage distribution of the population aged 15 years and over by marital status, sex and administrative division: 1990 census

Administrative division	Unmarried			Married			Widowed			Divorced		
	Both sexes	Male	Female	Both sexes	Male	Female	Both sexes	Male	Female	Both sexes	Male	Female
Sichuan	26.9	31.3	22.3	66.0	63.6	68.6	6.5	4.4	8.8	0.6	0.7	0.4
Henan	25.4	28.8	22.0	67.7	66.5	68.9	6.3	3.9	8.8	0.5	0.8	0.2
Shandong	23.8	26.6	20.9	69.5	68.9	70.2	6.3	3.9	8.7	0.4	0.5	0.2
Jiangsu	21.6	25.3	17.9	71.5	70.6	72.4	6.5	3.5	9.5	0.4	0.8	0.3
Guangdong	30.0	34.6	25.2	62.9	61.8	64.0	6.7	2.9	10.6	0.4	0.7	0.2
Hebei	21.1	24.2	17.8	72.3	70.9	73.8	6.1	4.2	8.1	0.5	0.8	0.2
Hunan	25.2	29.6	20.3	67.8	65.1	70.8	6.4	4.3	8.6	0.6	0.9	0.3
Anhui	27.7	31.6	23.4	65.7	63.7	67.7	6.2	3.8	8.7	0.5	0.8	0.2
Hubei	24.3	28.1	20.3	68.7	66.7	70.8	6.4	4.4	8.6	0.6	0.8	0.3
Zhejiang	24.3	28.8	19.5	68.6	66.7	70.6	6.4	2.2	9.6	0.6	1.0	0.2
Liaoning	21.1	23.9	18.1	73.2	71.7	74.6	5.0	3.5	6.6	0.7	1.2	0.8
Jiangxi	26.4	30.8	21.8	66.8	64.8	68.9	6.2	3.5	9.0	0.6	0.9	0.2
Yunnan	26.9	30.8	22.8	66.4	64.6	68.2	6.1	3.9	8.5	0.6	0.7	0.5
Heilongjiang	24.1	26.8	21.2	70.4	68.7	72.1	4.8	3.6	8.4	0.8	0.9	0.6
Shaanxi	24.2	28.2	19.8	69.4	66.8	72.2	8.4	4.1	7.7	0.6	0.9	0.3
Guizhou	28.8	32.4	24.8	64.7	62.4	67.1	6.0	2.3	7.8	0.6	0.8	0.3
Fujian	25.1	29.7	20.4	67.8	66.1	69.6	6.5	3.3	9.9	0.6	0.9	0.2
Shanxi	24.2	28.3	19.8	69.4	66.8	72.2	8.4	4.1	7.7	0.6	0.9	0.3
Jilin	22.7	25.3	19.8	71.5	69.8	73.2	5.1	3.8	8.7	0.8	1.0	0.6
Gansu	26.4	30.3	22.3	67.5	65.1	70.1	5.4	3.7	7.3	0.6	0.9	0.3
Hainan	28.4	33.5	23.0	64.9	62.9	67.1	6.1	2.7	9.7	0.6	0.8	0.3
Qinghai	29.7	33.9	25.1	64.2	62.0	66.5	5.0	3.0	7.2	1.2	1.1	1.2
Guangxi	28.9	33.9	23.6	63.9	61.4	66.7	6.5	3.9	9.4	0.6	0.9	0.3
Nei Mongol	26.4	30.1	22.5	68.2	65.4	71.2	4.8	3.7	5.9	0.6	0.8	0.3
Xinjiang Uygur	28.4	32.8	23.7	64.3	62.2	66.6	4.5	2.2	7.0	2.8	2.9	2.7
Ningxia Hui	27.1	30.2	23.8	68.2	66.5	70.0	4.2	2.6	5.8	0.5	0.6	0.4
Tibet	32.9	35.7	30.1	57.3	58.5	56.1	7.3	4.6	10.0	0.2	0.1	0.4
Shanghai	18.1	22.4	13.6	74.6	74.0	75.2	6.4	2.7	10.2	0.9	0.9	0.9
Beijing	22.1	25.9	18.1	72.2	70.7	73.8	5.0	2.7	7.4	0.7	0.7	0.7
Tianjin	19.3	21.9	16.6	74.7	74.4	75.2	5.5	3.3	7.7	0.6	0.6	0.5
China	25.1	29.0	21.1	68.2	66.4	70.0	6.1	3.8	8.5	0.6	0.8	0.3

Source: State Statistical Bureau, *1994 Statistical Yearbook of China*, pp. 62-63.

Table 18. Marital status distribution of the population aged 15 years and over by level of educational attainment and sex: 1990 census

(Percentage)

Educational level	Unmarried			Married			Widowed			Divorced		
	Both sexes	Male	Female	Both sexes	Male	Female	Both sexes	Male	Female	Both sexes	Male	Female
Illiterate and semi-illiterate	7.7	15.0	4.5	71.0	68.5	72.1	20.6	14.7	23.1	0.7	1.8	0.3
Primary school	24.5	25.7	23.0	71.5	69.2	74.0	3.4	4.1	2.6	0.6	1.0	0.3
Junior middle school	36.2	36.5	35.0	62.5	62.1	63.2	0.9	0.9	0.7	0.5	0.5	0.4
Senior middle school	31.0	31.2	30.8	67.8	67.7	67.9	0.6	0.6	0.6	0.6	0.5	0.6
Technical secondary school	31.1	29.1	33.9	67.4	69.7	64.2	0.9	0.7	1.3	0.5	0.5	0.6
Junior college	27.1	24.6	32.5	71.5	74.2	65.7	0.7	0.6	0.9	0.6	0.6	0.8
University	35.6	34.7	38.1	62.7	64.0	59.5	1.0	0.8	1.5	0.6	0.5	0.8
All educational levels	25.1	29.0	21.1	68.2	66.4	70.0	6.1	3.8	8.5	0.6	0.8	0.3

Source: State Statistical Bureau, *1994 Statistical Yearbook of China*, pp. 64-65.

of Chinese females exceeded that of Chinese males, but today the female mortality rate is lower than the male rate. Estimates based on the 1982 and 1990 census data indicate that the proportion of female deaths in the total number of deaths declined from 47.1 per cent in 1981 to 44.9 per cent in 1989, and that this decline has occurred in respect of female deaths at all age groups excepting the 0-4, 20-24 and 65-69 years (annex table C.4). In 1989, the overall death rate for females (5.46 per thousand) was lower than the rate for males (6.32 per thousand), and the female rate was also lower than the male rate at all age groups excepting at ages 0-4 years (table 19).

Table 19. Age-specific death rates by gender: 1989

Age group	Death rate (per thousand population)		
	Both sexes	Male	Female
0-4	6.35	6.11	6.61
5-9	0.73	0.84	0.61
10-14	0.59	0.67	0.50
15-19	0.98	1.08	0.87
20-24	1.17	1.41	1.17
25-29	1.27	1.40	1.12
30-34	0.75	1.72	1.29
35-39	0.98	2.24	1.60
40-44	1.43	3.29	2.30
45-49	4.30	5.02	3.50
50-54	6.85	8.04	5.52
55-59	10.94	13.10	8.54
60-64	18.47	22.38	14.37
65-69	26.22	35.99	23.26
70-74	48.69	59.15	39.75
75-79	71.72	86.79	60.51
80-84	136.41	149.13	99.16
85-89	160.00	190.52	145.73
90+	242.10	271.13	231.61
All ages	5.90	6.32	5.46

Source: Yao Xinwu and Yia Hua, *Basic Data of China's Population*, Data User Service Series No. 1 (China Population Publishing House).

(a) Maternal mortality

One of the most sensitive indicators of women's health is the maternal mortality rate, which is closely linked to the basic health of pregnant women and the health services available to them. While there is a specialized Maternal and Child Health Station at the county level (average population 400,000), facilities and equipment for MCH care at the village and township levels are often limited. Consequently, maternal care varies by region, with a prenatal coverage of about 98 per cent in the cities and 78 per cent in the countryside. In most cities, about 96 per cent of pregnant women have an average of five prenatal examinations. A study of 300 poor counties, however, found that only 37 per cent of pregnant women received antenatal care and 21 per cent received three or more visits. Generally, deliveries occur under strictly sterile conditions with full sterile conditions for mother, baby, midwife and medical instruments. In 1992, about 53 per cent of all deliveries in the country occurred in hospitals, the proportion in cities (71.7 per cent) being considerably higher than that in the countryside (41.2 per cent). In poor counties, only 14 per cent of the deliveries took place in a hospital setting and only 36 per cent had deliveries meeting hygienic standards.

Although comprehensive data on maternal mortality are not yet available, estimates based on surveys and hospital data indicate that China has progressed from extremely high rates in the 1940s (1,500 per 100,000 live births) to a current middle position with an estimated national rate of 95 per 100,000 in the late 1980s. However, there are marked variations in the maternal mortality rate between urban and rural areas and between various administrative regions. For instance, a 1989 study covering 100 million people in all 30 provinces, municipalities and autonomous regions reported a maternal mortality rate of 90 per 100,000 live births for the country as a whole, but the rate for rural areas (115) was more than double that for urban areas (50 per 100,000). The study also found serious under-reporting of maternal deaths (34 per cent) and of births (15 per cent). About 20,000 women die every year in China from maternal causes.

The 1989 study also reported that mortality rates were highest among women who had received little or no prenatal care and among those whose first prenatal visit took place later than 28 weeks' gestation. Women who delivered at home had a threefold risk of death compared with those who delivered in hospital (table 20).

Table 20. Maternal mortality rates and relative risk by number of prenatal visits, gestation time of first visits and place of delivery: 1989

Variable	Maternal mortality rate (per 100,000 live births)	Relative risk
Number of prenatal visits		
None	778	35
1-2	199	9
3-4	71	3
5-6	32	1
6+ (6+ = 1)	23	1
Gestation time of first visit		
< 12 weeks (< 12 = 1)	27	1
12-27 weeks	54	2
27+ weeks	71	3
Place of delivery		
Provincial hospital (=1)	23	1
County hospital	46	2
Village hospital	47	2
At home	113	5

Source: Carla Abou Zahr and Erica Royston, *Maternal Mortality. A Global Fact Book* (Geneva, World Health Organization, 1991).

The 1989 study referred to above also reported that compared with women aged 25-29 years, the risk of death owing to complications of pregnancy and puerperium was four times higher for women aged 15-19 years, seven times higher for those aged 35-39 years and 20 times higher for those 40 years and above. This risk was also 15 times higher for women with four or more children than for women having their first child (table 21).

According to the 1989 study, illiterate women were at greater risk of maternal death than women with primary-level or higher education; the maternal mortality rate among women with university-level education was only 5 per 100,000 live births, compared with 359 per 100,000 for illiterate women (table 22). However, a 1988/89 study carried out in 25 counties in Jiangsu Province and seven counties in Henan Province showed that widespread

Table 21. Maternal mortality rates and relative risk by age group and birth parity: 1989

Age group and birth parity	Maternal mortality rate (per 100,000 live births)	Relative risk
Age group		
15-19	196	4
20-24	64	1
25-29 (= 1)	50	1
30-34	125	3
35-39	360	7
40+	1 028	20
Parity		
Primiparous (= 1)	42	1
Parity 2	82	2
Parity 3	217	5
Parity 4+	634	15

Source: Carla Abou Zahr and Erica Royston, *Maternal Mortality. A Global Fact Book* (Geneva, World Health Organization, 1991).

Table 22. Maternal mortality rates and relative risk by socio-economic characteristics and geographic residence: 1989

Background characteristics	Maternal mortality rate (per 100,000 live births)	Relative risk
Literacy and education level		
Illiterate	359	67
Primary level education	124	23
Junior middle school	44	8
Higher middle school	21	4
University (= 1)	5	1
Family monthly income		
< 20 yuan	211	5
20-49 yuan	98	3
50-99 yuan	31	1
100+ yuan	36	1
Geographic residence		
Mountains	181	4
Plains (= 1)	46	1
Other	61	1

Source: Carla Abou Zahr and Erica Royston, *Maternal Mortality. A Global Fact Book* (Geneva, World Health Organization, 1991).

dissemination of health messages could offset the lack of education to some extent. Knowledge of a minimum of three health messages on the part of either husband or wife was found to be positively correlated with the use of prenatal care services and delivery in county hospitals.

The level of family income is an important determinant of the level of maternal mortality rate because income affects the socio-economic situation of the family as well as the nutritional status of the mother. Generally, women from poor families tend to have more children than those from well-to-do families and are thus exposed to a higher risk of maternal death. According to the 1989 study, the maternal mortality rate was highest (211 per 100,000 births) among families with monthly incomes of less than 20 yuan, and lower among families with monthly incomes exceeding 50 yuan. The rate was also found to be about four times higher in mountainous areas than in the plains (table 22).

The various national as well as regional-level studies have generally confirmed that post-partum haemorrhage is the single most important cause of maternal mortality, accounting for 47 per cent of all maternal deaths in the 1984-1988 survey of 21 of the 30 administrative regions; 60 per cent of all maternal deaths in Henan and 46 per cent in Jiangsu according to the 1988/89 study of these two provinces;

and 49 per cent of all maternal deaths, according to the 1989 study of all 30 provinces, municipalities and autonomous regions (table 23).

The factors contributing to the high mortality from post-partum haemorrhage are lack of adequate care, including screening and referral of high-risk women for hospital delivery, proper management of labour and delivery, and provision for emergency transport, treatment and blood transfusion at township clinics and village health stations and with private doctors. The staff at township clinics and village health stations are not sufficiently trained to deal with emergencies, and women with complications reporting to these institutions often face inordinate delays in being transferred to the hospital, mainly because the staff cannot realize the gravity of the situation and take immediate action. In particular, they lack the skills to prevent and manage post-partum haemorrhage, to check blood types and to organize local "walking blood banks". Further, over half of women who die in poor counties do so at home, and nearly half had no trained medical attention in the 24 hours before death. Morbidity both in pregnancy and among women in general is not as well studied as mortality. Non-fatal complications of delivery, such as post-partum fever, occur, but are better managed

Table 23. Percentage distribution of maternal deaths by major cause: 1984-1988, 1985-1987, 1988-1989 and 1989 studies

Major cause	1984-1988[a/]	1985-1987[b/] urban areas	1988-1989[c/] Henan	1988-1989[c/] Jiangsu	1989[d/]
Haemorrhage	47	12	60	46	49
Hypertensive disorders of pregnancy	10	4	10	11	10
Cardiac diseases	10	13	–	–	9
Gipsies	5	7	11	4	6
Embolism	5	7	1	1	5
Ectopic pregnancy	1	9	–	7	–
Rupture of the uterus	–	1	3	–	–
Hepatitis	4	9	–	–	4
Other	18	38	15	39	17
All causes	100	100	100	100	100

Source: Carla Abou Zahr and Erica Royston, *Maternal Mortality. A Global Fact Book* (Geneva, World Health Organization, 1991).

[a/] Cross-sectional study covering 21 of the total 30 administrative divisions.
[b/] Data for Shanghai Municipality.
[c/] Covering 25 countries in Jiangsu Province and seven countries in Henan Province.
[d/] Covering all 30 administrative divisions.

owing to the availability of antibiotics. Severe complications such as uterine prolapse or fistula are very uncommon, owing to better care and a greatly reduced number of deliveries per woman. Iron deficiency anaemia has been found in half or more of pregnant women in rural areas.

Aside from promoting scientific methods of child delivery, the main efforts in the area of women's health have been directed towards the prevention and treatment of cervical cancer in urban areas, and a general survey and treatment of prolapse and vesicolvaginal fistula in rural areas.

(b) Infant and child mortality

In China, the infant mortality rate (IMR) is estimated to have declined from around 200 per 1,000 live births in the 1930s and 1940s to 40-50 per 1,000 live births in the 1980s (figure 4). The degree of decline is unprecedented for such a large and developing country. The national rates of fewer than 35 reported from the 1982 and 1990 population censuses are generally considered to be underestimated. For instance, the 1989-1990 IMR derived from the 1990 census data was only 27.3 per 1,000 live births for the country as a whole (annex table C.5). According to recent estimates prepared by the United Nations, the declining trend in IMR in China had slowed in the 1980s, but had declined significantly from 50 in 1985-1990 to 44 in 1990-1995 (table 24). Neonatal morta-

Figure 4. Trends in infant mortality rate: 1950-1987

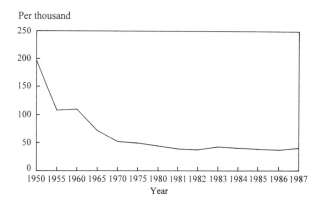

Source: China Population Information and Research Centre.

lity is estimated to account for about 50-75 per cent of all infant deaths, depending on the source.

The infant mortality rate, like the maternal mortality rate, varies markedly across the 30 administrative divisions, between urban and rural areas, and between males and females. According to estimates based on the 1990 census data, IMR varied from a low of 8.8 in Beijing Municipality to a high of 96.2 in Tibet. In general, infant mortality rates are higher in remote, mountainous and less developed areas, and among the minority groups that tend to inhabit these areas. In practically all provinces and autonomous regions, rural IMR was substantially higher than urban IMR, and in several provinces the rural rate was two to three times the urban rate. In most provinces, female IMR was significantly higher than male IMR; in the

Table 24. Trends in infant mortality and life expectancy at birth: 1950-1955 to 1990-1995

Period	Infant mortality rate	Life expectancy at birth (years)		
		Both sexes	Male	Female
1950-1955	195	40.8	39.3	42.3
1955-1960	179	44.6	43.1	46.2
1960-1965	121	49.5	48.7	50.4
1965-1970	81	59.6	58.8	60.4
1970-1975	61	63.2	62.5	63.9
1975-1980	52	65.3	64.4	66.3
1980-1985	52	66.6	65.5	67.7
1985-1990	50	67.1	65.8	68.4
1990-1995	44	68.5	66.7	70.4

Source: United Nations, *World Population Prospects: The 1994 Revision.*

municipalities, IMR for males exceeded that of females (annex table C.5).

Although comprehensive information on the causes of infant mortality is not available on a nationwide basis, relatively reliable data on major causes of infant mortality are available from various studies for Shanghai county (representing low IMR areas), 17 selected rural counties (representing moderate IMR areas), and 300 remote counties (representing perhaps the poorest 25 per cent of China, or high IMR areas). The data from these studies are summarized in table 25.

It is clear from table 25 that the major causes of infant deaths in China are problems of the newborn, acute respiratory infection (ARI), tetanus and diarrhoea. In the 300 remote counties with a high mortality rate as well as in the 17 selected rural counties with moderate rates of infant mortality, the most important or frequent cause appears to be pneumonia, but the experience of Shanghai county indicates that deaths due to pneumonia could be reduced to low levels. Although neonatal tetanus was earlier considered to have been virtually eliminated, it appears to be still an important and completely preventable cause of infant death. National surveys conducted in 1987 revealed tetanus as causing 1.4 to 4 deaths per thousand live births.

Among children between one and five years, the main causes of death are acute respiratory infections (pneumonia), diarrhoea and injuries. A picture of the major causes of death of children under 5 years, obtained by combining data relating to infant (under one year) and child (1-4 years) deaths, is given in table 26.

It will be noted from table 26 that ARI accounts for about one fourth of all deaths among children under 5 years of age. Data from other sources (not included in table 26) indicate that 40 per cent of pneumonia deaths in

Table 26. Numerical and percentage distribution of deaths among children under 5 years of age by major cause: 1989

Major cause	Number of deaths (thousands)	Percentage
Diarrhoea	140	10.0
Immunizable diseases[a]	100	7.1
[Neonatal tetanus][b]	[98]	[–]
ARI/pneumonia	340	24.3
Others	820	58.6
Neonatal[c]	340	24.3
Accidents/injuries	150	10.7
Other	330	23.6
All causes	1 400	100.0

Source: UNICEF, "An analysis of the situation of children and women in China" (draft) (Beijing, August 1992).

[a] Measles, pertussis, diphtheria, polio, tuberculosis, tetanus.
[b] Included in neonatal deaths.
[c] Prematurity/low birthweight, birth trauma, asphyxia, cold injury.

Table 25. Causes of infant mortality in selected sites and years

(Per thousand live births)

Cause of infant mortality	300 remote counties (1989)	17 selected rural counties (1982-1985)	Shanghai county (1980)
Pneumonia	17	10	3
Prematurity	10	5	4
Birth trauma, asphyxia, cold injury	12	6	3
Neonatal tetanus	6	n.a.	n.a.
Congenital	5	4	6
Injuries	4	3	1
Diarrhoea	6	2	n.a.
Others	8	3	2
Total	68	33	19

Source: UNICEF, "An analysis of the situation of children and women in China" (draft) (Beijing, August 1992).

n.a. = not available or insignificant number.

children occur during the first month of life. These sources also reveal that China's diarrhoea rate of two episodes per year for children under 5 years is similar to global rates, but the case fatality rates are very low, resulting in few deaths. As is evident from table 26, diarrhoea accounts for only 10 per cent of the deaths among children under 5 and this relatively low fatality rate is attributed to improved nutrition, the cultural practice of giving starchy gruels to children with diarrhoea, and a widespread primary health care network. The incidence of diarrhoea is quite high in rural areas during the first two years of life, probably related to the early introduction of fluids or food other than breastmilk, and poor hygienic conditions at home.

A major success has been in the reduction of deaths due to immunizable or vaccine preventable diseases. In 1981, China joined the World Health Organization (WHO)-coordinated Expanded Programme on Immunization (EPI) against tuberculosis, diphtheria, pertussis, tetanus, polio and measles. The government provided political and financial support for immunization services at every level and initiated major efforts to expand coverage. During the 1980s, the government as well as international organizations also made large investments in the transport and refrigeration facilities with the objective of establishing a "cold chain" for vaccines, allowing for at least six vaccination sessions per year, even in poor rural areas.

As a result of the various measures adopted, coverage of the four basic vaccines (BCG, polio, DPT and measles) reached 80 per cent in each province by 1988 and 80 per cent in nearly all counties by 1990 (with an average county level of 95 per cent). According to the preliminary results of the National Child Survey published by the State Statistical Bureau in 1994, immunization coverage at the national level was 90 per cent for BCG, 88 per cent for polio, 86 per cent for DPT and 85 per cent for measles, the coverage rate in urban areas being significantly higher than in rural areas in respect of each of the four vaccines (table 27). A recent statement issued by the Information Office of the State Council of the People's Republic of China and published in the *Beijing Review* of January 1996 reported that the percentage of children inoculated with BCG, measles and polio vaccine was 93.96, 89.37 and 93.74 respectively.

On account of the progress made in regard to immunization coverage, there has been a dramatic reduction in the incidence of major diseases. Between 1978 and 1993, for every 100,000 population, pertussis decreased from 126 to 1, diphtheria from 2 to 0.01, and measles from 250 to 10. Exceptions include outbreaks of polio in certain locations in 1989 and 1990, which began to taper off in 1991. Investigation by officials of the Ministry of Public Health and United Nations agencies following the outbreak showed that most of the children affected were incompletely immunized and mostly belonged to the floating or unregistered populations in the outbreak locations. As a result of special campaigns, polio cases were reduced by two thirds in the period 1992-1994.

The improvement in the health status is reflected not only in the decline in maternal and infant mortality rates but also in the rise in life expectancy. As will be noted from table

Table 27. **Immunization coverage for four basic vaccines by urban and rural areas and selected provinces**

				(Percentage)
Area/province	BCG	Polio	DPT	Measles
China	90	88	86	85
Urban	95	94	93	85
Rural	85	86	84	73
Shanxi	65	66	62	49
Guizhou	72	74	67	53

Source: State Statistical Bureau, *Preliminary Results of National Child Survey,* 1994.

24, the average life expectancy at birth increased remarkably for both males and females between 1950-1955 and 1990-1995, and during these 40 years, female expectancy has been consistently higher than male expectancy. The 1990-1995 female expectancy of 70.4 years is 3.7 years longer than the male expectancy. The overall maternal and child health status in China for exceeds that of most developing countries and compares well with middle-income countries.

3. Educational background

Since the founding of the People's Republic in 1949, there has been a rapid increase in participation at all levels of education as well as in the educational attainment of both males and females. This had resulted in a significant reduction in the marked educational inequality that had existed before liberation between males and females as well as between various regions in the country. The increase in the educational levels of women over the years has largely been due to a series of measures adopted by the government to encourage girls to attend schools and to change the attitudes of parents towards the education of their daughters.

Despite major national efforts and the substantial progress made, there are still significant disparities in enrolments and participation rates as well as in the level of educational attainment between males and females, between the developed and underdeveloped regions, between rural and urban areas, and between the majority Han population and the various minority nationalities.

(a) Educational participation

(i) Basic education

An important aspect of educational development in China during the past four decades has been the sustained efforts at providing opportunities for basic education to all children, youth and adults. The progress achieved by China in this respect is indeed very impressive compared with most other developing countries.

Available data indicate that there were generally considerable increases in student enrolments at pre-school, primary and junior secondary levels between 1960 and 1990 (table 28). At the pre-school or kindergarten level, the number of students enrolled increased steadily, from 11.51 million in 1980 to 19.72 million in 1990. The average enrolment rate for all 3-6 year-old children in three-year kindergartens and one-year pre-school classes was about 28 per cent, and girls constituted about 48 per cent of all kindergarten enrolments in 1990.

It is also evident from table 28 that the number of students enrolled at primary and junior secondary levels declined between 1980 and 1990. This decline was due to a reduction in the number of children in the eligible age groups resulting from drastic fall in fertility rates. Over the years, the proportionate share

Table 28. Student enrolments in kindergartens (pre-school), primary and junior secondary schools: 1960-1990

Year	Kindergartens (pre-school)		Primary schools		Junior secondary schools	
	Number (millions)	Percentage girls	Number (millions)	Percentage girls	Number (millions)	Percentage girls
1960	29.33	–	93.79	39	8.59	–
1980	11.51	–	146.27	45	45.84	40
1986	16.29	47	131.83	45	41.17	–
1987	18.08	47	128.36	45	42.62	40
1988	18.55	47	125.36	46	40.16	41
1989	18.48	46	123.73	46	38.38	42
1990	19.72	48	122.41	46	38.69	43

Source: UNICEF, "An analysis of the situation of children and women in China" (draft) (Beijing, August 1992).

of girls in total enrolments has increased from 39 to 46 per cent at the primary level and from 40 to 43 per cent at the junior secondary level. It is also clear that while girls progress to higher educational levels, their proportion in total enrolments decreases steadily at each level; in 1990, girls constituted 48 per cent of enrolments at the kindergarten level, 46 per cent in primary schools and 43 per cent in junior secondary schools.

According to official statistics, the primary enrolment ratio, or percentage of 7-11-year-old children in primary schools, increased from 20 per cent in 1949 to 96 per cent in 1990. But a 1992 Sample Survey on the Situation of Chinese Children showed that the enrolment ratio for all children aged 7-11 years was 91.6 per cent, with the ratio for girls (89.7 per cent) being 3.7 percentage points less than the ratio of 93.4 per cent reported for boys. The Survey also revealed that these enrolment ratios varied not only between rural and urban areas but also within these two areas, depending either on the geographical location or the size of the settlements. For example, the female enrolment ratio averaged 87.6 per cent in rural areas but was 96.6 per cent in urban areas; the urban female enrolment rate was almost equivalent to the urban male rate and higher than the average male rate for the country. Within rural areas, the female enrolment ratio was lowest (82.3 per cent) in mountainous areas and highest (90.9 per cent) in the plains. Within urban areas, the female enrolment ratio increased with the increase in the size of urban area; this ratio ranged from 94.3 per cent in townships to 98.4 per cent in big cities. In all areas and localities, the enrolment ratio for boys was higher than the corresponding ratio for girls (table 29).

While considerable progress has been made in regard to the education of girls, about 70 per cent of an estimated 3.6 million children aged 7-11 years who are not enrolled in schools are girls, particularly from rural and remote mountainous areas and from minority nationality groups. The main reason for this low participation is economic: poor parents keep their girls at home to help with income-generating activities, and school fees also constitute a substan-

Table 29. School enrolment ratios of children aged 7-11 years by residence and sex: 1991/92 school year

Residence	Both sexes	Boys	Girls
China	91.6	93.4	89.7
Rural areas	90.1	92.3	87.6
Flatland	92.2	93.3	90.9
Hills	91.7	92.9	90.4
Mountains	86.6	90.9	82.3
Urban areas	96.7	96.8	96.6
Big cities	98.5	98.6	98.4
Medium cities	96.3	96.9	96.0
Small cities	95.5	95.7	95.3
Townships	94.5	94.6	94.3

Source: State Statistical Bureau, *Sample Survey on the Situation of Chinese Children* (July 1992).

tial claim on the low incomes of the poor families. Another reason is the influence of the lingering feudal idea on the part of some rural parents that males are superior to females. This kind of attitude is prevalent not only among some minority nationalities but also in some remote Han-nationality populated areas.

In the absence of relevant data, it is not possible to determine the drop-out rates at primary and junior secondary levels precisely. However, estimates seem to suggest that the drop-out problem is quite serious in China because several families find it difficult or are not willing to pay the increased tuition fees and educational levies. Another important factor is that the opportunity costs of child and teenage labour are increasing with the financial incentives of the economic reforms. In 1988, the Vice Minister of the State Education Commission indicated that 3.3 per cent of all primary school pupils and 6.4 per cent of all junior secondary school students, amounting to about 7.15 million children, had dropped out of school. He noted that apart from economic reasons, the drop-out problem was due to other factors, such as lack of relevance of the curriculum to the needs and environmental contexts of the learners, poor quality of teaching, and unsatisfactory physical facilities and learning environment in schools.

An analysis of the data relating to children aged 6-14 years who were not attending school as on July 1990 indicated that of the 10.6 million children aged 7-11 years, corresponding to primary school age, about 6.1 million, or 57.5 per cent, were girls. It is likely that of the 6.1 million girls not attending school, over half were enrolled but for various reasons not attending. The analysis also showed that the overall non-attendance rate at ages 7-11 years was 12.9 per cent for girls and only 8.7 per cent for boys. At the primary level, the non-attendance rate was highest at age 7, or the first grade, with 26.6 per cent of girls as against 22.4 per cent of boys reported as not attending. The analysis also indicated that at all ages, the non-attendance rate for girls was considerably higher than the corresponding rates for boys. At age 14 years or final year of junior secondary, the non-attendance rate for girls (36.7 per cent) was over 1.6 times that of 22.4 per cent reported for boys (table 30).

However, according to the 1992 Sample Survey on the Situation of Chinese Children, the drop-out rate at the national level was higher for boys than for girls at grades 1 and 5, and lower than or equal to that of girls at other grades. But the pattern differed between urban and rural areas. While the pattern obtaining in rural areas was similar to the national pattern, in the urban areas the drop-out rate for girls was higher than the rate for boys at grades 1, 2 and 4 and lower than that of boys for other grades. The Survey also revealed that the drop-out rates of urban girls were considerably higher than those of rural girls at grades 1 and 4 (table 31).

Table 30. Percentage of children aged 6-14 years not attending school by single year of age and sex: 1 July 1990

Age	Percentage of children not attending school		
	Both sexes	Male	Female
6	58.8	57.4	60.3
7	24.4	22.4	26.6
8	9.1	7.3	11.2
9	6.3	4.4	8.2
10	5.7	3.7	7.8
11	7.3	4.9	9.9
12	12.1	8.5	16.0
13	18.7	13.3	24.4
14	29.3	22.4	36.7
6-14	19.1	16.0	22.3
7-11	10.7	8.7	12.9

Source: UNICEF, "An analysis of the situation of children and women in China" (draft) (Beijing, August 1992).

Note: Data relate to school attendance of children on 1 July 1990 and not to enrolment status at the beginning of the school year 1989/90.

The 1992 Sample Survey on the Situation of Chinese Children also revealed that illness and disability together constitute the major reason for urban children dropping out of school: 55.8 per cent of female drop-outs and 52.5 per cent of male drop-outs gave these reasons. But in the rural areas the majority of boys as well as girls who dropped out did so for economic reasons, that is, family economic difficulties and for assisting with household activities: 50.5 per cent of the girls and 36.7 per cent of the boys who dropped out reported these reasons. The second most important

Table 31. Percentage distribution of drop-out students at primary level by grade, sex and residence: 1991/92 school year

Grade	China		Urban		Rural	
	Male	Female	Male	Female	Male	Female
1	36.6	32.3	21.7	42.1	37.8	31.9
2	20.2	22.3	8.7	10.5	21.1	22.7
3	19.3	21.2	43.5	15.8	17.4	21.4
4	13.7	13.7	17.4	21.1	13.4	13.5
5	9.3	8.5	8.7	5.3	9.4	8.6
6	0.9	2.0	–	5.3	1.0	1.9

Source: State Statistical Bureau, *Sample Survey on the Situation of Chinese Children* (July 1992).

reason for dropping out of school was disability in the case of rural girls (32.0 per cent) and illness in the case of rural boys (10.0 per cent). Difficulty with studies was a very significant reason why both boys and girls dropped out in rural as well as urban areas. As is to be expected, the transport problem was a more important reason in rural than in urban areas (table 32).

(ii) Secondary and tertiary education

China has also made considerable progress in regard to enhancing women's participation in secondary and tertiary education. Prior to the founding of the People's Republic, women constituted only around 20 per cent of total enrolments in secondary schools and vocational training institutions, and about 18 per cent of all students in institutions of higher learning (colleges and universities). Since the early 1950s, there has been a tremendous increase in the number of females enrolled at various institutions of middle and tertiary education. By 1994, females accounted for about 44 per cent of all students attending regular secondary schools; about 49 per cent of students in specialized secondary schools; about 48 per cent of students enrolled in vocational schools; and approximately 35 per cent of students at institutions of higher learning. In other words, the relative share of females in total enrolments in various types of secondary and tertiary educational institutions had either

doubled or more than doubled during the past 50 years (table 33).

An important factor contributing to the increasing participation of females at all levels of education is the increase in the number and proportion of female teachers in the country. Data from official sources indicate that between 1978 and 1994, the percentage of female teachers in the total number of teachers has shown a steady increase at all levels of education in China. During this period, the proportionate share of women in the total number of teachers had increased from 37.8 to 45.8 per cent in primary schools; from 24.4 to 34.7 per cent in regular secondary schools; from 27.3 to 41.3 per cent in specialized secondary schools; and from 25.2 to 32.1 per cent in institutions of higher education. The relative share of female teachers in vocational middle schools almost trebled, from 13.0 per cent in 1980 to 35.7 per cent, in 1994 (table 34).

(b) Educational attainment

Although the participation of women in various levels of education had increased very substantially during the past four decades, their overall educational attainment and literacy level remains much lower than that of men. Data from the censuses indicate that the average number of years of education received by females aged 6 years and over had increased from 3.5 years in 1982 to 4.6 years in 1990.

Table 32. Percentage distribution of drop-out children (7-11 years) by reasons for dropping out of school, sex and residence: 1991/92 school year

Reason for dropping out	Urban areas		Rural areas	
	Male	Female	Male	Female
Illness	36.4	39.4	10.0	5.2
Disability	16.1	16.4	6.1	32.0
Family economic difficulty	10.7	5.1	29.3	40.2
Help with domestic chores	2.9	2.2	7.4	10.3
Difficulty with studies	6.6	4.8	8.0	6.4
Unsatisfactory school facilities	3.7	0.7	1.6	1.2
Transport problem	0.4	0.4	2.1	2.3
Not enough teachers	–	–	1.0	0.6
Other reasons	23.1	30.9	34.5	1.8
All reasons	100.0	100.0	100.0	100.0

Source: State Statistical Bureau, *Sample Survey on the Situation of Chinese Children* (July 1992).

Table 33. Percentage of female students in secondary and tertiary level educational institutions: 1952-1994

Year/period	Percentage of female students			
	Regular secondary schools	Specialized secondary schools	Vocational schools	Institutions of higher studies
Before liberation	20.0	21.4	–	17.6
1952	23.5	25.0	–	23.4
1957	30.8	26.5	–	23.3
1965	32.2	40.5	23.6	26.9
1978	41.5	33.1	–	24.2
1980	39.6	31.5	32.6	23.4
1985	40.2	38.6	41.6	30.0
1990	41.9	45.4	45.3	33.7
1992	43.4	45.9	46.0	34.2
1993	43.7	47.4	46.7	33.6
1994	44.3	48.8	47.8	34.5

Sources: Wei Zhangling, *Status of Women: China* (UNESCO, 1989); and State Statistical Bureau, *1995 Statistical Yearbook of China.*

Table 34. Percentage of female teachers in total number of teachers at various levels of education: 1978-1994

Type of school/institution	1978	1980	1985	1990	1992	1993	1994
Primary schools	37.8	37.1	39.6	43.2	44.5	45.2	45.8
Regular secondary schools	24.4	24.8	28.1	31.5	33.3	34.0	34.7
Specialized secondary schools	27.3	26.6	32.8	38.0	39.6	40.6	41.3
Vocational middle schools	–	13.0	24.8	31.5	33.5	34.4	35.7
Institutions of higher education	25.2	25.5	26.7	29.1	29.9	30.9	32.1
All educational institutions	32.5	32.4	35.2	38.4	39.8	40.5	41.2

Source: State Statistical Bureau, *1995 Statistical Yearbook of China.*

Yet in 1990, females aged 6 years and over received on an average 1.6 years less education compared with their male counterparts. This gender disparity in the length of schooling is reflected in the gap in educational attainment between males and females in China.

According to the 1990 census, a significantly higher proportion among males than among females aged 15 years and over had completed junior middle school or higher education. While the proportion of those who had completed primary education was about the same for males (35.3 per cent) and for females (33.8 per cent), the proportion among males completing junior middle school (36.0 per cent) was about 12 percentage points higher than

the corresponding proportion of 24.3 per cent reported for females (table 35).

It is also clear from table 35 that women represent a disproportionate share of the illiterate and semi-illiterate population. Among the 817.4 million persons aged 15 years and over in 1990, about 181.6 million, or 22.2 per cent, were reported as illiterate or semi-illiterate; and of the 181.6 million illiterate or semi-illiterate, 127.2 million, or 70 per cent, were women. In other words, the number of female illiterates was more than twice that of male illiterates. Illiterate and semi-illiterate women constituted about 32 per cent of all women aged 15 years and over, the corresponding proportion for men being only 13 per cent.

Table 35. Numerical and percentage distribution of persons aged 15 years and over by level of educational attainment and sex: 1990 census

Level of educational attainment	Both sexes		Male		Female	
	Number (million)	Percent-age	Number (million)	Percent-age	Number (million)	Percent-age
Illiterate and semi-illiterate	181.6	22.2	54.4	13.0	127.2	31.9
Primary school	282.5	34.6	147.8	35.3	134.7	33.8
Junior middle school	247.8	30.3	151.0	36.0	96.8	24.3
Senior middle school	72.5	8.9	44.6	10.6	27.9	7.0
Technical secondary school	17.3	2.1	10.1	2.4	7.2	1.8
Junior college	9.6	1.2	6.6	1.6	3.0	0.8
University	6.1	0.7	4.4	1.1	1.7	0.4
All levels	817.4	100.0	418.9	100.0	398.5	100.0

Source: State Statistical Bureau, *1994 Statistical Yearbook of China.*

The age-specific illiteracy and semi-illiteracy rates given in table 36 show that these rates for both males and females increase with advancing age, reflecting historical patterns in regard to the availability of educational opportunities. It is also evident from table 36 that the female illiteracy rates are higher than the male rates in all age groups, but this difference is smaller at the younger than at the older ages. This indicates marked improvements in female educational attainment but at the same time implies that much remains to be done in order to eliminate gender differences in educational opportunities.

The national average illiteracy and semi-illiteracy rate conceals the marked variation in these rates between the 30 administrative divisions of the country. Both in 1982 and 1990, these rates for females were substantially higher than the male rates in all provinces, autonomous regions and municipalities. In 1990, illiteracy and semi-illiteracy rates for females aged 15 years and over ranged from a low of 16.6 in Liaoning and 16.9 in Beijing to a high of 83.1 per cent in Tibet, and the female rate was lower than the national average of 31.9 per cent in all three municipalities, in the autonomous regions of Guangxi, Nei Mongol and Xinjiang Uygur, and in eight provinces. The 1990 female adult illiteracy and semi-illiteracy rate exceeded 50 per cent in five provinces: Guizhou (53.2 per cent); Yunnan (51.2 per cent); Tibet (83.1 per cent); Gansu (53.1 per cent) and Qinghai (54.4 per cent). Female illiterates and semi-illiterates also constituted 45.1 and 48.3 per cent of all females aged 15 years and over in Ningxia and Anhui provinces respectively in 1990 (annex table C.6).

Table 36. Percentage of illiterates and semi-illiterates by age group and sex: 1982 and 1990 censuses

Age group	1982 census			1990 census		
	Both sexes	Male	Female	Both sexes	Male	Female
15-24	11.23	4.79	17.90	5.72	3.02	8.55
25-34	24.08	11.16	37.95	9.29	3.92	15.03
35-44	33.06	18.06	49.96	18.47	9.12	28.57
45 and over	67.29	46.94	87.77	52.42	33.61	71.65
Total	34.49	20.81	48.86	22.21	12.98	31.93

Source: Government of China, *The Second Report of the People's Republic of China on the Implementation of the Nairobi Forward-looking Strategies for the Advancement of Women* (Beijing, February 1994).

D. WOMEN IN FAMILY LIFE

1. The Chinese family

In China, as in most countries of the world, the family constitutes the most important basic unit of social and economic life, serving as the traditional institution for reproduction and child-rearing, and as a source of emotional support and vehicle for socialization of its members. Over the past 2,000 years or more, the extended family has been the single most important social institution in China. This family type, which was more or less coextensive with a localized patrilineage, comprised the patrilineal grandparents, their unmarried children and all of the married sons and their families, and functioned as a coordinated income and consumption unit. The family structure, however, differed according to the social class. While the extended family was more typical of the gentry or élite, the nuclear family, consisting of a man, his wife and their unmarried children, was more common among the peasantry.

The traditional Chinese family reckoned its descent in the male line, and within the family, relationship among members was based on the supremacy of males over females and of age over youth. In other words, sex and age were regarded as the only two factors determining an individual's place within the hierarchical structure of the family. The head of the family was always a male: the father in a nuclear family, and the oldest male of the senior generation, usually the paternal grandfather, in the extended family. The family head enjoyed absolute authority representing his family in dealings with other families as well as with the State, and his decisions were binding on all members of the household.

The family name and property were handed down from father to son; occasionally widows held land on behalf of their infant sons, though it was usual to entrust the land to a male relative of the dead father so that it could be worked by a male. Daughters had no inheritance rights because upon marriage they would leave their parental homes and become completely a part of their husband's families. It was only in an exceptional situation, when the family had no male offspring and opted to continue the line of descent by keeping the daughter at home and arranging an uxorial marriage for her, that the land was passed through the female line. Generally, women could not inherit property either as wives or as daughters. Sons were therefore considered important and were desired most intensely to ensure the continuity of the family.

The traditional family system also required the wife to be submissive to her husband's authority and bear his children, particularly male offspring. If she produced only daughters or if she was infertile, the husband was free to take a second wife or a concubine, or both, to give himself a male heir. Upon the death of her husband, the wife was usually not permitted to remarry but had to submit to the authority of his family or of his eldest son who became the new family head. Although the remarriage of widows was not part of the ideal of the traditional Chinese family system, it was a normal practice among the peasants in some areas, particularly if the widow was young.

The ideals of the traditional family were achieved at the expense of female members who, as noted earlier, were relegated to a very low status within the system. To begin with, the birth of a girl was never as welcome as that of a boy and might have been considered a tragedy in a poor family or in one with no male offspring. Women were required not only to be submissive and obedient to their husbands but also to show deference to all males within and outside the family. They had no authority or say in the management of important family matters and could not participate as individuals in social, political or economic activities. Even in regard to choosing their marriage partners, women had no freedom but merely obeyed the dictates of their parents and heeded the words of the matchmakers. They were secluded within the home and mostly performed household chores, although in poorer families women often helped the men in cultivation. By and large, women were subjected to physical and mental torture, being harassed by systems of polygamy and prostitution.

However, the values of the traditional family system came to be questioned or challenged with the introduction of Western cultural influences in the latter part of the nineteenth century. At the beginning of the present century, the growth of manufacturing industries and the consequent formation of a new labour force that was independent of patrilineal sponsorship, together with increasing urbanization, provided greater opportunities, especially to the young persons, for social relationships outside the restricted family circle. Demands for reforms gradually began to emerge, resulting in the formation of the new Republic of China in 1912. The 1920s and 1930s witnessed popular agitation for liberating women from the restrictions of the past and for giving young men and women greater freedom, social mobility and the right to participation in social, economic and political affairs.

Although these movements achieved few practical results, they succeeded in focusing public attention on the need to reform the traditional family system and emphasized the importance of the nuclear family as a basic social unit and, within it, greater freedom for women and children. The Kinship Relations Law promulgated in 1930 embodied most of the demands for reform, but its direct impact on Chinese society as a whole was very limited for lack of effective enforcement. Changes, however, did take place among the urbanized and partly Westernized groups during the Sino-Japanese war (1937-1945), and the new family model was carried to other parts of the country by refugees from the coastal cities.

The lives of Chinese women began to change following the founding of the People's Republic in 1949. Committed as it was to the achievement of female emancipation and equality between men and women, the government of the People's Republic adopted a series of legislative and other measures aimed at eradicating the antiquated system and outmoded customs that fettered, discriminated against and humiliated women. The relevant laws and administrative actions that have come into force since 1949 to enhance the status of women are discussed in various sections of this profile.

Consequent on the enforcement and implementation of various laws and administrative measures, today Chinese women enjoy, at least theoretically, the same rights as men in regard to access to education, health and other welfare services; ownership of property and inheritance; and participation in political and economic life. In particular, special attention has been paid to protecting women's rights in marriage and the family, and to guaranteeing in law women's independence in marriage, equal rights between husband and wife in decision-making and the management of family affairs. A recent survey revealed that in 58 per cent of the families in China, decisions concerning important family matters are made jointly by the husband and wife. Abuse of a wife by her husband or a daughter-in-law being ill-treated by mother-in-law or father-in-law are considered unacceptable in society.

The social changes that have swept the country in recent decades have also resulted in significant changes in the size and structure of families or households. The Chinese Regulations for Household Registration recognize two types of household: the domestic household, or registration unit of families residing in a township or a rural district, and the collective household, or the registration unit for those living in collective dormitories of civic or governmental institutions, enterprises etc. The analysis and discussion that follow in this section relate only to domestic households.

Estimates based on data from various official sources (table 37) show that the average household size during the pre-liberation years had remained more or less stable at 5.17 to 5.38 persons. From 5.35 in 1947, the average household size had declined to 4.30 at the 1953 census. This sharp decline was largely due to the fact that the land reforms introduced at the beginning of the 1950s had resulted in a break-up of several large, particularly more than three-generation, families into many smaller nuclear families, resulting in an increase in the number of households by about 47 million, from 86,637,312 in 1947 to 133,845,988 in 1953. The decline in the rate of natural increase of the population during the early years

Table 37. Average size of domestic households: 1911-1993

Year	Source of data	Average household size (persons)
1911	1934 *Economic Yearbook* of China	5.17
1912	Statistics from the Ministry of Internal Affairs	5.31
1928	Statistics from the Ministry of Internal Affiairs	5.27
1933	Statistical abstracts	5.29
1936	Reports of the Ministry of Internal Affairs	5.38
1947	Statistics of the Bureau of Population	5.35
1953	National population census	4.30
1964	National population census	4.29
1982	National population census	4.43
1990	National population census	3.97
1993	National sample survey on population	3.90

Sources: Ma Xia, "An analysis of the size of domestic household and the family in China", in Li Chengru and others, eds., *A Census of One Billion People*, papers for the International Seminar on China's 1982 Population Census, 26-31 March 1984 (Beijing, April 1984); Jiang Zhenghua and Zeng Yi, "Family size, structure and child development", in *Family Planning, Health and Family Well Being*, Proceedings of the United Nations Expert Group Meeting on Family Planning, Health and Family Well Being, Bangalore, India, 26-30 October 1992 (New York, 1996) (ST/ESA/SER.R/131); and State Statistical Bureau, *1994 Statistical Yearbook of China.*

of the 1960s led to a further shrinkage in average household size to 4.29 at the 1964 census.

According to the 1982 census, the average household or family size was 4.43 persons, or an increase of 0.14 persons over the 1964 average size. The increase is somewhat surprising in view of the fact that socio-economic conditions had improved and fertility had declined substantially between 1964 and 1982. The reported increase in family/household size during this period has therefore to be attributed largely to the serious housing shortage which occurred during the Cultural Revolution (1966-1976), resulting in several smaller families living with large families. Since 1982, the average family size had declined to 3.97 at the 1990 census and further to 3.90 in 1993, according to the National Sample Survey on Population. These declines can be explained in terms of an increase in the number of small families with one or two children as well as improvements in the housing supply in the 1980s.

Data from the four national censuses from 1953 to 1990 also show that the average family size was larger in rural than in urban areas, except in 1953, when the average urban family size was larger than that of the rural family (table 38). The relatively smaller average size

Table 38. Average family size in China by urban and rural residence: 1953-1990

Census year	Average family size (number of persons)		
	China	Urban	Rural
1953	4.30	4.66	4.26
1964	4.29	4.11	4.35
1982	4.43	3.95	4.57
1990	3.97	3.55	4.14

Source: Jiang Zhenghua and Zeng Yi, "Family size, structure and child development", in *Family Planning, Health and Family Well Being,* Proceedings of the United Nations Expert Group Meeting on Family Planning, Health and Family Well Being, Bangalore, India, 26-30 October 1992 (New York, 1996) (ST/ESA/SER.R/131).

of the rural family in 1953 was due to the break-up of large families into smaller ones following the dramatic changes in land and property ownership introduced at the beginning of the 1950s. It is also evident from table 38 that between 1953 and 1982 the average family size increased in the rural areas and decreased in the urban areas. These changes were due to two important factors: a sharper decline in fertility in urban than in rural areas during this period, and the greater persistence in rural than in urban areas of the traditional custom of parents living with one married child. In 1982 as well as in 1990, the urban family was significantly smaller than the rural family.

The average family size also varied significantly across the 30 administrative divisions of the country in both 1982 and 1990 (annex table D.1). Between 1982 and 1990, the average family size had declined in all divisions excepting in two autonomous regions, Xinjiang and Tibet, which exhibited slight increases in family size. In 1990, the average family size was smaller than the national average in all three municipalities and in 10 of the 22 provinces. In the other 12 provinces and the five autonomous regions, family size ranged from a low of 4.0 in Nei Mongol to a high of 5.20 in Tibet. By and large, the average family size was larger in remote border provinces and in some national minority areas, reflecting the differences in levels of socio-economic development, in cultural norms and practices and in the practice of family planning.

Over the years, there has also been a tendency towards nuclearization of families or a change from larger to small families. Data from various sources indicate that the proportion of households with five or more persons each had declined from about 55 per cent in the 1930s to about 46 per cent in 1982 and further to about 31 per cent in 1993. Consequently, the proportion of small households/families with four or less than four persons had increased from about 45 per cent in the 1930s to about 69 per cent in 1993 (table 39).

In 1990, the proportion of households with four or less than four persons was higher than the national average of 69 per cent in 15 of the 30 administrative divisions of the country. While this proportion constituted 84 per cent or higher in the three municipalities of Shanghai, Beijing and Tianjin, households with five or more persons were typical in provinces such as Guangdong, Guangxi, Qinghai and Hainan (annex table D.2).

Data from the censuses also indicate changes in family structure or type between 1982 and 1990. The tendency by the newly married younger generation to set up their own households has resulted in an increase in the proportionate share of one-couple (husband and wife) families, from 4.8 per cent in 1982 to 6.5 per cent in 1990, and the increase in this proportion was more marked in large cities and towns than in rural areas. Along with this development, there has been a decrease in the proportion of families with one generation and other relatives and non-relatives, from 1.2 per cent in 1982 to 0.8 per cent in 1990, the extent of decline being about the same in rural and urban areas. While families with two generations and other relatives and non-relatives constituted more than two thirds of all families in 1982 and 1990, the three-generation family is still an important family type

Table 39. Percentage distribution of households by household size: 1931, 1982 and 1993

Year	Household size (number of persons)								
	1	2	3	4	5	6	7	8 and over	Total
1931	2.5	8.3	15.4	19.0	17.9	13.0	8.8	15.1	100.0
1982	7.9	10.1	16.1	19.6	18.4	13.1	7.9	6.9	100.0
1993	5.9	11.2	26.2	25.8	16.4	7.8	3.6	3.1	100.0

Sources: 1931: Professor Buck, in a survey of 22 provinces, cited in Ma Xia, "An analysis of the size of domestic household and the family structure in China", table 5, in *A Census of One Billion People,* papers for the International Seminar on China's 1982 Population Census, 26-31 March 1984 (Beijing, April 1984).

1982: National population census, 1982.

1993: National sample survey on population, 1993.

in China, accounting for a little less than 20 per cent of all families in the country (table 40).

2. Family formation

(a) Marriage practices and patterns

Traditionally, Chinese have regarded marriage and stable family life as a basic quality of life, and hence marriage rates had been very high, with only a negligible proportion of adult men and women remaining single for ever. Early and universal marriage was pervasive because, in their anxiety to have their children settled and thus ensure their posterity, parents always arranged their children's marriages early if they could afford to do so. Available studies report that between 1921 and 1930, about 81 per cent of women marrying for the first time were below 20 years of age.

Generally, the parents of both the bride and the groom had to incur considerable expenditure when their children married. When the bride moved to her groom's house after marriage, she had to take with her a dowry, the nature and value of which varied according to the social class and region. Among the wealthy families, the dowry was usually in the form of jewellery, while among the poor it consisted of clothing, bedding and household items for use by the newly married couple. In most cases, the value of the dowry was expected to be higher than the value of the gifts which the groom's parents had sent to the bride's parents. On the whole, the bride price and wedding expenses were much higher in the countryside than in the cities.

Another form of marriage which was common in many rural areas was one in which the future daughter-in-law was adopted as a small child into the house of her in-laws. This arrangement, which several anthropologists referred to as "minor marriage" as opposed to the more orthodox "major marriage", was more prevalent among the poor since it helped to reduce considerably the expenses related to the marriage ceremony. This arrangement was also acceptable to the groom's parents as they were assured of a more amenable daughter-in-law with strong ties of affection with them. However, the system was hard on the girls, who had to be separated from their parents and siblings at an early age.

Whatever the type of marriage contracted, its primary function in traditional Chinese society was perceived to be the production of male offspring to ensure the continuity of the family line, and this perception therefore largely dictated the way in which marriages were arranged. Over 95 per cent of the marriages were arranged by parents or senior members of the family without consulting and obtaining the consent of the bride and groom because the interests of the family as a whole were more important than the likes and dislikes of the two individuals concerned.

The system of arranged marriages was particularly disadvantageous to the young bride

Table 40. Percentage distribution of families by type and residence: 1982 and 1990

Family type	1982				1990			
	China	City	Town	Rural	China	City	Town	Rural
One-person	8.0	9.3	11.3	7.5	6.3	7.0	7.8	5.9
One-couple	4.8	5.7	5.7	4.5	6.5	8.2	8.0	5.8
One generation and other relatives etc.	1.2	1.7	1.8	1.1	0.8	1.2	1.2	0.7
Two generations and other relatives etc.	67.3	67.2	67.7	67.3	68.1	67.2	68.5	68.2
Three generations or more	18.7	16.1	13.5	19.7	18.5	16.5	14.4	19.4
All types	100.0	100.0	100.0	100.0	100.0	100.0	100.0	100.0

Source: Jiang Zhenghua and Zeng Yi, "Family size, structure and child development", in *Family Planning, Health and Family Well Being,* Proceedings of the United Nations Expert Group Meeting on Family Planning, Health and Family Well Being, Bangalore, India, 26-30 October 1992 (New York, 1996) (ST/ESA/SER.R/131).

who had to move to her husband's home after marriage, often in another village. Since her contacts and social interactions hitherto had been limited to her own family and village, she had to enter her husband's family as a stranger and adjust herself to new surroundings, become subordinate to all senior members of that family, and at times even dominated by the younger members in the family. She was also required to be obedient to her parents-in-law, and had to be careful to avoid any friction with her mother-in-law who would be both her workmate and supervisor. Besides serving her mother-in-law at meals, the daughter-in-law also had to take over from her mother-in-law the most arduous and unpleasant of the household chores.

The stressful phase of married life would, however, be over and respect accorded to the daughter-in-law once she gave birth to a son. But if the couple had no male offspring, she would be blamed for the misfortune and, as noted earlier, the husband would be free to take a concubine to give himself a male heir, although this alternative was beyond the means of many families. When the husband took a concubine, the lot of the wife would be still harder, since she had to put up with both a sense of personal failure and the reproaches of others for the rest of her life. Thus, in the China of the past, women were victims of early marriage and treated as childbearing tools, often ill-treated by their parents-in-law or abandoned by their husbands because they were unable to provide any offspring, let alone a son.

However, dramatic changes in the concept and patterns of marriage began to take place in China with the promulgation in 1950 of the Marriage Law of the People's Republic of China. The fundamental principles of this law, which was also aimed at improving the status of women in the country, were that the marriage system should be based on the free choice of both partners, on monogamy, and on equal rights for both sexes. The law expressly prohibited concubinage and polygamy, child betrothal, and interference with the remarriage of widows. Bride price and the exaction of money or gifts in connection with marriage were made illegal. It also stipulated medical conditions for marriage and established the mi-

nimum age for marriage at 18 years for women and 20 years for men, or about the same as the normal age at marriage in the pre-liberation era.

The government also launched vigorous campaigns to publicize and enforce the 1950 Marriage Law which, together with land reform, constituted the major theme of all propaganda for social reforms. All means of mass communication, newspapers, magazines, special booklets, comic strips, stories, posters, leaflets, drama troupes and the radio, were used to educate all sections of the population on the evils of the old system and the virtues of the new. Despite these efforts, implementation remained unsatisfactory, and investigations revealed that a substantial number of arranged marriages still took place without the consent of the couples concerned during the early 1950s. After 1953, further efforts were made to publicize and enforce the 1950 Marriage Law, and the average age at marriage of women increased to 19 years, although a significant minority of village women continued to marry at a younger age.

During the 1970s, the Government strongly encouraged late marriages as a means of reducing fertility. The "wan-xi-shao" policy stressed late marriages (wan), longer intervals between births (xi) and fewer children (shao). The national family planning programme tried to raise the age of marriage by controlling the issuance of marriage permits; it became increasingly difficult to obtain permission to marry if the marrying couple did not meet the minimum age requirements stipulated by the programme, usually 23 years for women and 25 years for men. Consequently, the female age at marriage is estimated to have increased to about 23 years by 1980. Estimates also indicate that first marriages of women under age 18 as a proportion of total marriages in the country had declined from about 48.3 per cent in 1955 to 16.3 per cent in 1970 and further to 6.2 per cent in 1980 (table 41).

Although efforts were made to increase the minimum age of marriage through local regulations to 25 years or higher for men and 23 years or more for women, these efforts proved to be very unpopular and resulted in

Table 41. Percentage of first marriage of women under 18 years of age: 1945-1980

Area	1945	1950	1955	1960	1965	1970	1975	1980
China	40.3	40.6	48.3	28.8	26.4	16.2	5.9	6.2
Urban	39.7	39.7	29.2	19.9	15.1	10.2	7.2	2.1
Rural	40.4	40.9	34.6	31.0	28.6	17.6	6.5	7.3

Source: Peng Peiyun, "The population of China: problems and strategy", *China Population Today*, vol. 9, No. 4, 1992.

an increase in the number of unregistered marriages. In response to this negative reaction, the Chinese Fifth National People's Congress adopted a new Marriage Law in September 1980 which, while retaining the principles of the 1950 law, set the minimum legal age of marriage at 20 for women and 23 for men. Although these minimum ages were higher than those set in the 1950 law, they were still lower than the guidelines imposed by the family planning programme during the 1970s.

While the Government had continued to promote late marriages, estimates indicate that the mean age at first marriage of Chinese women declined somewhat in the 1980s from 22.84 years in 1980 to 22.18 years in 1988 (table 42) perhaps owing to the publicity given in 1981 to the raising of the minimum legal age of marriage for women from 18 to 20 years, which revealed to many Chinese that the much advocated 23 years for late marriage was not indeed the legal minimum. It is also clear from table 42 that in 1988 women in rural China still married in their early 20s, while in urban areas women did not marry until their mid-20s.

Estimates also indicate that the mean age at first marriage for Chinese women has increased continuously since 1988, reaching 22.6 years in 1992. This increase has been attributed to an increase in the number of deferred marriages (marrying after 25 years for men and after 23 years for women) and a decline in the number of early marriages (marrying before the legal minimum age of 22 years for males and 20 years for females). These in turn have largely been due to the tightening up of the implementation of the late marriage regulations.

According to the data from the 1990 census, 98.2 per cent of males and 95.3 per cent of females aged 15-19 years remained never married, but the proportion never married declines rapidly with age, and was 62.5 per cent for males and 41.4 per cent for females at ages 20-24 years. Nearly 96 per cent of females and 83 per cent of males were married by the time they were 25-29 years old. The 1990 census data also show that the proportion of never-married women is positively related to education for all age groups. It is also interesting to note that a greater proportion of women

Table 42. Standardized average age at first marriage of Chinese women by urban and rural residence: selected years, 1970-1988

Area	1970	1980	1982	1984	1986	1987	1988
China	20.82	22.84	22.41	22.28	22.13	22.16	22.18
Urban	22.92	25.37	24.66	24.38	24.05	24.10	24.04
Rural	20.24	22.13	21.77	21.63	21.56	21.53	21.60

Source: Peng Peiyun, "The population of China: problems and strategy", *China Population Today*, vol. 9, No. 4, 1992.

than men aged 30 years and over with vocational or college education were reported to be never married (table 43).

Despite the stipulation of a legal minimum age at marriage, data from censuses and other sources indicate that the number of men and women marrying before the legal minimum age, 22 years for men and 20 years for women, has been increasing in recent years. Early marriages have been commonly observed in Chinese rural areas since the late 1980s; in 1987, there were six provinces and autonomous regions where the mean age at first marriage was lower than the legally stipulated minimum. The number of women aged 15-19 years who were reported to be married increased from 2.664 million at the 1982 census to 2.727 million at the 1992 census, while the number of males aged 15-21 years reported as married increased from 1.760 million in 1982 to 5.736 million in 1990. Estimates prepared by the Department of Civil Affairs indicate that the number of persons marrying before the legal minimum age accounted for more than 20 per cent of all marriages annually in recent years.

Thus, early marriages remain an important demographic phenomenon in China. Such marriages not only violate the Marriage Law but also have an adverse impact on the implementation of the family planning programme. Besides, early marriages and early childbearing are harmful to women and children physically and psychologically. In some backward and remote areas, early marriages also result in such abuses

as child betrothal, which is prohibited by the country's laws.

It must, however, be noted that over the past four decades, Chinese women have increasingly exercised their legally guaranteed right of self-determination in marriage or freedom in choosing their partners in life. Sample investigations show that 74 per cent of couples make the decision themselves to wed, or do so after consultation with their parents, and that 80 per cent of marriages of women under 40 years of age are based on their own choice. These proportions are, of course, higher in urban than in rural areas, and higher among more educated than less educated persons.

(b) Reproductive behaviour

During the past four decades, there have been great changes, not only in marriage practices and patterns but also in the reproductive behaviour of the Chinese people. During these 40 years, the fertility pattern underwent a radical transformation from one of relatively early childbearing, short birth-spacing, and many births typical of most developing countries to one of late childbearing, longer birth intervals and few births characteristic of developed countries. In other words, Chinese women's childbearing has, by and large, changed from the spontaneous, unplanned state to a conscious and planned one.

During the first half of the 1950s, China experienced very high fertility rates; the official estimates place the crude birth rate at about

Table 43. Percentage of population never married by educational level and sex for selected age groups: 1990 census

Eucational level	Males by age group						Females by age group					
	15-19	20-24	25-29	30-34	35+	15+	15-19	20-24	25-29	30-34	35+	15+
Illiterate or semi-illiterate	95.1	66.5	40.1	26.0	8.4	15.0	87.3	24.6	2.4	0.5	0.2	4.5
Primary	97.6	60.8	21.6	10.8	4.2	25.7	93.8	35.0	2.5	0.2	0.1	23.1
Junior high	98.4	57.1	13.3	4.8	2.0	36.5	97.3	42.4	4.2	0.6	0.4	35.7
Senior high	99.6	76.0	14.0	3.5	1.5	31.2	99.4	66.0	6.8	1.3	0.8	30.8
Vocational school	99.8	84.5	22.7	2.6	0.6	27.3	99.7	74.5	13.3	3.0	0.9	33.5
College	100.0	94.6	35.8	5.5	0.7	34.7	100.0	88.7	22.0	7.2	1.5	38.1
All levels	98.2	62.5	16.7	7.2	4.4	29.0	95.3	41.4	4.3	0.6	0.2	21.1

Source: Li Rose Maria and Susan F. Newcomer, "The exclusion of never-married women from Chinese fertility surveys", *Studies in Family Planning*, vol. 27, No.3, May/June 1996.

37-38 per thousand population and the total fertility rate at about six children per woman (table 44). This high fertility pattern resulted from a combination of several factors. First, the rapid expansion of agricultural and industrial production and the resultant improvement in people's living standards that followed the founding of the People's Republic provided a conducive environment for rearing large families. Second, in the absence of any radical changes in traditional methods of cultivation, children continued to contribute to farm labour without much training and were therefore still regarded as a source of wealth by their peasant parents. Third, the pronounced cultural preference of parents to have several sons that had existed in the country for thousands of years was still persistent. Fourth, the decline in infant mortality rates which had just begun had not been adequate to convince parents to change their traditional desire for many children in order to ensure the survival of at least a few of them. Further, in the early stages of the People's Republic, official policy was in favour of increasing population in keeping with the standard Marxist theory that over-population cannot exist in a communist state where wealth is equally allocated.

However, during the period of economic difficulty associated with the "Great Leap Forward", the crude birth rate declined substantially, from about 38 per thousand in 1954 to about 25 in 1959 and to a historic low of 18 per thousand in 1961. Thereafter, the birth rate began to rise again, reaching 43.4 in 1963, when TFR was estimated at 7.5, and then declined gradually to 33.4 per thousand population in 1970. The 1970s witnessed a dramatic reduction in the fertility rates, with the crude birth rate declining by about 47 per cent from 33.43 in 1970 to 17.82 in 1979 and TFR declining by about 53 per cent from 5.81 to 2.75 children per woman during the same period. Since 1980, the fertility rates have been fluctuating at a low level and in 1991 official estimates give a crude birth rate of 19.68 per thousand population and TFR of 2.07 (table 44 and figure 5).

After two decades of decline, fertility in China has now reached replacement level but,

Table 44. Crude birth rates and total fertility rates: 1949-1992

Year	CBR	TFR	Year	CBR	TFR
1949	36.00	–	1971	30.65	5.44
1950	37.00	5.81	1972	29.77	4.98
1951	37.80	5.70	1973	27.93	4.53
1952	37.00	6.47	1974	24.82	4.16
1953	37.00	6.05	1975	23.01	3.58
1954	37.97	6.28	1976	19.91	3.24
1955	32.60	6.26	1977	18.93	2.84
1956	31.90	5.85	1978	18.25	2.73
1957	34.03	6.41	1979	17.82	2.75
1958	29.22	5.68	1980	18.21	2.26
1959	24.78	4.30	1981	20.91	2.61
1960	20.86	4.02	1982	22.28	2.86
1961	18.02	3.29	1983	20.19	2.42
1962	37.01	6.02	1984	19.90	2.35
1963	43.37	7.50	1985	21.04	2.20
1964	39.14	6.18	1986	22.43	2.42
1965	37.88	6.08	1987	23.33	2.59
1966	35.05	6.26	1988	22.37	2.52
1967	33.96	5.31	1989	21.53	2.35
1968	35.59	6.45	1990	21.06	2.31
1969	34.11	5.72	1991	19.68	2.20
1970	33.43	5.81	1992	18.24	2.00

Source: Peng Peiyun, "The population of China: problems and strategy", *China Population Today*, vol. 9, No. 4, 1992; and The State Family Planning Commission of China, *Population Problém and Family Planning in China* (October 1993).

Note: The figures given in this table are official estimates and do not necessarily tally with the United Nations quinquennial estimates given in table 4 of this profile.

Figure 5. Total fertility rate for China: 1950-1992

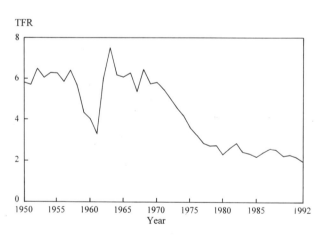

Source: The State Family Planning Commission of China, *Population Problem and Family Planning in China* (October 1993).

as noted earlier, the bulk of this decline had occurred in the 1970s before the introduction of the one-child policy. The decline in fertility as had occurred, particularly in the 1970s, had been unprecedented in speed and magnitude, and this reduction was achieved largely through the increased use of modern contraceptives. The standstill in fertility decline in the 1980s was largely due to the fact that the fertility rate had already reached a very low level at the beginning of the 1980s and there was very little potential for a further decline. Moreover, the switch-over of the population policy from "deferred, spaced but fewer births" to the "advocacy for one child per couple" required a greater effort for family planning implementation.

There are, however, substantial differences in the timing and extent of fertility decline among the various administrative divisions of the country. A recent study based on the data from the 1982 One-per-Thousand Fertility Sampling Survey, and from the 1988 Two-per-Thousand Fertility and Birth Control Sampling Survey covering 28 provinces, autonomous regions and municipalities, showed that although fertility rates had declined in all 28 administrative divisions between 1973 and 1977, the magnitude of the decline in each division had an evident association with the initial or previous fertility level. The study reported that, compared with the previous level, there was a relatively larger magnitude of decline in 14 divisions, among which Sichuan, Shanxi and Heilongjiang were outstanding examples; a smaller magnitude of decline in seven other divisions, including Guangdong, Ningxia, Qinghai and Anhui; and no value difference in the remaining seven administrative divisions. The study also showed that, between 1978 and 1987, there was a continued decline in fertility rates in 22 administrative divisions, while there was a rise in these rates in the other six divisions, namely, Jiangsu, Shaanxi, Hubei, Shandong, Sichuan and Shanghai (annex table D.3).

As noted earlier, family planning had played a very crucial role in the fertility decline over the past three decades. With the steep decline in mortality during the 1950s and the consequent rapid growth of the population, the government recognized the need for organized family planning services to enhance maternal and child health, improve women's status and moderate the rate of growth of the population for accelerating socio-economic development. The Contraceptives and Induced Abortion Procedures Act of 1953 legalized the import and sale of contraceptives, and legalized sterilization and abortion with certain restrictions; this law was further liberalized in 1957. The 1982 Constitution of the People's Republic of China, the country's most important legal document, affirms the importance of family planning to curb population growth and confirms that it is the duty of both wife and husband to practise family planning. The 1984 Drug Control Law requires strict guidelines for the safety of contraceptive drugs and devices. The 1991 Decision on Strengthening the Family Planning Programme to Strictly Control Population Growth contains provisions suggesting the use of IUDs, sterilization and abortion in specified circumstances.

During the initial stages, family planning activities had to be limited to the cities in China, on account of a shortage of trained health personnel and facilities in the rural areas. Even these limited efforts were disrupted during the "Great Leap Forward" in the late 1950s, the disastrous famines in the early 1960s and during the political turmoil associated with the Cultural Revolution in the mid-1960s. Vigorous family planning efforts, however, began in 1971 when the government incorporated efforts to slow population growth into overall economic planning. In 1973, the government introduced the *"wan-xi-shao"* policy campaign advocating delayed marriage, a four-year interval between births and two children per couple. In 1974, the State Council's Leading Group for Family Planning issued a circular stating that contraceptives should be issued free of charge. In the early 1970s, some areas instituted a process of birth planning in which annual targets for births were established at the national and provincial levels and, in principle, translated into numbers of approved births at lower administrative levels. The "later, sparser, fewer" theme remained the dominant family planning theme up until 1979.

In June 1979, the State Council recommended the provisions of incentives and rewards to couples giving birth to only one child, and in 1980, the Fifth National People's Congress adopted a general call for "only one child per couple". This shift in official policy was precipitated by the realization that, given the age structure of the population, even an average family size of two children would generate continuing population growth for decades to come. In terms of the new policy, married couples who have one child and promise not to have any more receive one-child certificates that entitle them to special benefits, such as monthly stipends and extended maternity leave. Although only limited exceptions to the one-child family policy were envisioned initially, since 1984 revisions of provincial family planning regulations have generally expanded the categories of couples that qualify for approval of a second child. Despite exemptions, the one-child policy remains the cornerstone of China's family planning policies and laws.

Since the 1980s, publicity and educational units, set up in all family planning committees at the provincial and municipal levels, have been active in popularizing family planning policies and disseminating knowledge about childbearing and contraception. The extensive information, education and communication efforts have enabled an increasing number of couples to learn and obtain scientific knowledge about family planning. The 1987 China's In-depth Fertility Survey, covering one municipality and five provinces, revealed that knowledge of contraception was widespread and that the majority of married women knew of at least one contraceptive method, and that in different localities some had knowledge about several contraceptive methods. The Survey also showed that, in general, people had a better understanding of long-acting, safe and reliable methods such as IUD and sterilization than they did about traditional methods such as withdrawal and the so-called "safe period" (table 45).

Over the years, the proportion of couples in childbearing ages using effective contraception has also been increasing; according to official estimates, the contraceptive prevalence rate was 71.2 per cent in 1988, comparable with rates in most industrialized countries of the world. The contraceptive prevalence rate is estimated to have increased to 83.4 per cent in 1993. Data for the period 1988-1992 indicate that IUD and female sterilization, two highly effective methods, are the most widely used methods. In 1992, these methods together accounted for 78.7 per cent of all contraceptive methods used in China; this proportion ranks among the highest in the Asian and Pacific region. While about 12 per cent of the users resorted to male sterilization, the importance of other methods, such as pills, condom and spermicide, had been decreasing between 1988 and 1992 (table 46).

The pattern of contraceptive use also varies significantly among the country's administrative divisions. Although, at the national level, the vast majority of acceptors depend on IUDs and female sterilization, the use of condoms and reliance on abortion are by and large higher in urban than in rural areas. An analysis of the percentage of currently married women using contraception based on the data from the 1988 Two-per-Thousand Fertility and Birth Control Sampling Survey indicated that the use of sterilization (including vasectomy and tubal ligations) ranged at from a low of 11.2 per cent in Guangxi

Table 45. Percentage of married women who have ever heard of a contraceptive method: 1987

	Beijing	Liaoning	Shandong	Guangdong	Guizhou	Gansu
Oral pills	99	91	69	60	53	56
IUD	98	99	97	94	92	94
Other female methods	66	46	22	23	13	14
Condom	96	92	63	53	32	35
Withdrawal	51	37	10	18	11	8
Calendar	61	42	17	24	13	11
Injectable	63	49	25	31	32	35
Sterilization						
Female	97	98	98	97	95	96
Male	96	91	96	95	94	67

Source: National report on China's In-depth Fertility Survey 1987, cited in *China Population Today*, vol. 11, No. 3, 1994, Special Issue for the International Conference on Population and Development, Cairo, 1994.

Table 46. Percentage distribution of family planning acceptors by contraceptive method: 1988-1992

Contraceptive method	1988	1989	1990	1991	1992
Male sterilization	11.4	11.6	11.8	12.1	12.1
Female sterilization	36.1	36.6	37.4	38.9	39.6
IUD	41.1	41.1	40.6	39.0	39.1
Pills	5.8	5.4	5.0	4.8	4.1
Condom	4.0	3.8	3.7	3.9	3.9
Spermicide	0.9	0.8	0.9	0.8	1.2
Others	0.7	0.7	0.6	0.5	–
All methods	100.0	100.0	100.0	100.0	100.0

Source: Department of Planning and Statistics of the State Family Planning Commission, cited in *China Population Today*, vol. 11, No. 3, 1994, Special Issue for the International Conference on Population and Development Cairo, 1994.

Province to a high of 63.2 per cent in Fujian Province and that this proportion exceeded 50 per cent in 13 of the 29 provinces, municipalities and autonomous regions covered by the analysis. It also revealed that the proportion of users depending on methods other than sterilization and IUD was more than 40 per cent in Ningxia and Xinjiang but less than 5 per cent in Shaanxi, Henan, Sichuan, Guangdong and Hainan provinces. The use of user-controlled methods (oral pills, condoms, spermicide and IUDs) appears to be higher and the use of sterilization relatively lower in more developed administrative divisions such as Beijing, Tianjin and Shanghai, and less developed divisions with a higher proportion of ethnic minority populations such as Qinghai, Ningxia, Xinjiang, Yunnan, Guangxi and Guizhou (annex table D.4), suggesting that the more developed and the less developed parts of the country may have similar patterns of contraceptive use.

In order to analyse the relationship between levels of socio-economic development and the pattern of contraceptive use, the study based on the 1988 Sample Survey constructed a socio-economic index (SES) for each province. This index was derived as a composite of seven variables: percentage of adult literacy; primary and secondary school enrolment ratio; expectation of life at birth; infant survival rate; percentage of the male labour force not in agriculture; gross provincial product per capita; and percentage

of urban population. Based on the SES score, the provinces were classified into three groups, representing high development (SES rank 1), middle development (SES rank 2), and low development (SES rank 3). It will be noted from annex table D.4 that 9 provinces fall under high development, 10 under middle development, and another 9 under low development categories.

The pattern of contraceptive use by SES regions presented in figure 6 shows that this pattern is almost similar in the most and in the least developed provinces, and distinctly different in provinces with middle levels of socio-economic development. A relatively high percentage of couples use IUD and other user-controlled methods in most developed (60 per cent) and least developed (66 per cent) provinces, while in provinces with middle-level socio-economic development 57 per cent of the couples depend on sterilization.

The analysis of the pattern of contraceptive use by birth order indicates that around 79 per cent of women who have had only one child were using IUDs, and that sterilization was chosen only after the birth of second or higher order parity children. However, the proportion of women with two children who had undergone sterilization was 47.8 per cent in the most developed regions (SES 1) and 62.4 per cent in provinces with middle levels of development (SES 2), but only 16.0 per cent in least developed regions (SES 3). While in SES 1 and SES 2, the proportion of women with three or more children opting for sterilization was 61.6 and 58.4 per cent respectively, this proportion was again very low, 27.1 per cent, in SES 3, suggesting that either emphasis on and facilities for sterilization are limited in SES 3 regions or there exists a strong desire for more children and hence stronger resistance to sterilization in these areas. The analysis also showed that, on average, few men with only one child had a vasectomy or male sterilization and that hardly any married men in the most developed provinces had undergone sterilization, regardless of the number of children they had (table 47).

The changes in the reproductive behaviour of Chinese women that have taken place over the past few decades are also reflected in

Figure 6. Patterns of contraceptive use by socio-economic index regions of China: 1988

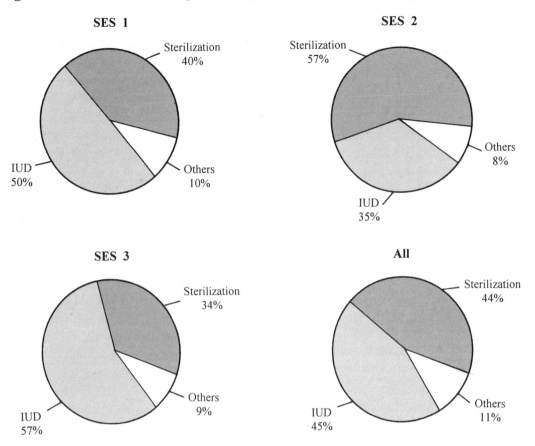

Source: Quanhe Yang, "Provincial patterns of contraceptive use in China", *Asia-Pacific Population Journal,* vol. 9, No. 4, 1994.

Table 47. Percentage of currently married women using contraception by method and birth order in different socio-economic regions: 1988

Region	Birth order	Sterilization		IUD	Pill	Condom	Others	All methods
		Male	Female					
SES 1	1 child	–	0.6	78.0	8.2	10.2	3.0	100.0
	2 children	0.4	47.8	42.7	4.8	2.7	1.6	100.0
	3+children	–	61.6	36.7	1.7	–	–	100.0
	Total	0.1	39.5	50.5	4.7	3.8	1.4	100.0
SES 2	1 child	0.3	1.5	78.8	9.3	5.8	4.3	100.0
	2 children	13.9	62.4	20.1	2.3	0.5	0.8	100.0
	3+children	24.7	58.4	14.7	1.6	–	0.6	100.0
	Total	14.2	43.5	34.8	4.0	1.8	1.7	100.0
SES 3	1 child	1.1	1.6	79.3	7.0	6.3	4.7	100.0
	2 children	20.2	16.0	56.2	5.2	0.6	1.8	100.0
	3+children	11.0	27.2	54.9	5.3	–	1.6	100.0
	Total	12.6	19.6	57.7	5.7	2.2	2.2	100.0
All regions	1 child	0.4	1.3	78.6	8.6	7.0	4.1	100.0
	2 children	13.3	52.5	29.2	3.1	0.8	1.1	100.0
	3+children	19.7	51.4	25.6	2.5	–	0.8	100.0
	Total	6.7	37.2	43.8	6.3	3.6	2.4	100.0

Source: Quanhe Yang, "Provincial patterns of contraceptive use in China", *Asia-Pacific Population Journal*, vol. 9, No. 4, 1994.

changes in the relative share of birth orders. During the 1940s, infants of third or higher parities accounted for 40-50 per cent of all births. Since the founding of the People's Republic, this proportion increased further, reaching about 62 per cent in 1970. Since the 1970s, with the increasing practice of family planning, the proportion of births at parities three and above had declined rapidly, reaching 12.8 per cent in 1991. Concomitantly, there has been an increase in the proportion of first births, from 20.7 per cent in 1970 to 53.4 per cent in 1991, and of second births, from 17.1 per cent to 33.8 per cent, during the same period (table 48). These trends clearly indicate that the policies and programmes to promote fewer births have been remarkably successful in China.

Table 48. Composition of birth orders in China: 1970-1991

Year	Percentage share of birth parity[a]		
	First	Second	Third and higher
1970	20.7	17.1	62.2
1977	30.9	24.6	44.5
1980	44.2	28.4	27.4
1982	50.6	26.1	23.3
1984	51.9	28.2	19.9
1986	50.7	32.7	16.6
1983	52.2	32.4	15.4
1989	51.9	32.5	15.6
1990	52.8	33.7	13.5
1991	53.4	33.8	12.8

Source: Peng Peiyun. "The population of China: problems and strategy", *China Population Today*, vol. 9, No. 4, 1992.

[a] The figures are mostly estimates based on family planning records or on sample surveys.

National averages, however, conceal the wide variations in percentage composition of birth orders among the 30 administrative divisions of the country. Estimates based on the data of the 1982 and 1990 population censuses show that between 1981 and 1991 the percentage share of first order births had increased in all administrative divisions excepting in two municipalities (Beijing and Tianjin) and in five provinces, Henan, Shandong, Hubei, Shaanxi and Shanxi, where this proportion had actually declined during the eight-year period. In 1989, the proportion of first order births averaged 49.4 per cent for the country as a whole, but ranged from a low of 25.0 per cent in Tibet to a high of 92.1 in Shanghai. This proportion was also lower than the national average in 16 provinces and 4 autonomous regions. Also in 1989, second order births constituted more than a third of all births in seven provinces, and the Guanxi Autonomous Region, while multiple births (third and higher order) constituted the majority of births in Tibet (54.7 per cent), Xinjiang (45.1 per cent) and about a third of all births in Guizhou and Hainan (annex table D.5).

An interesting development in regard to the reproductive behaviour of Chinese married couples during the past few decades has been the shortening of the interval between marriage and the couple's first birth. Several studies have shown that, prior to 1970, the mean length of first birth interval was well over two and a half years for all couples, and over three years for rural couples. This observed long first birth interval is rather surprising given the traditional cultural norms under which newly married couples are expected to have children soon after marriage to continue the family line. Strong social pressure was therefore exerted on the couple to have a child, especially a son, as early as possible. Besides, the use of contraception, particularly immediately following marriage, was then very low. It has, however, been suggested that the observed long interval between marriage and first birth may have resulted from obeying traditional restraints on coital frequency and that the co-residence of bride and groom delayed for several years may have depressed fertility early in marriage.

Analysis of data from censuses and surveys indicates that the first birth interval has been narrowing from about 34 months in the 1950s to less than 18 months in the early 1980s. According to the September 1982 Fertility and Family Planning Survey, the proportion of marriages experiencing a birth during the first year rose from 5 per cent of marriages entered in 1957 to 8 per cent in 1970 and to 12 per cent in 1980, while the proportion exhibiting a birth within the first three years of marriage rose from 38 per cent in 1957 to 52 per cent in 1970 and to 67 per cent in 1980. Analysis of the data from the 1982 and 1990 population censuses (annex table D.6) indicates that the gap between female mean age at first marriage and mean age at first birth declined by 1.79 years from 2.93 years in 1981 to 1.14 years in 1989. This analysis also showed that a shortening of the first birth interval between 1981 and 1989 had occurred in all administrative divisions of the country excepting the municipality of Shanghai, where it increased from 1.49 years to 2.60 years during this period. Further, in 1989, the first birth interval was less than the national average (1.14 years) in 13 provinces and 3 autonomous regions, and was only 0.51 years in Guangdong, 0.90 years in Qinghai and 0.95 years in Guizhou provinces.

All available studies confirm that the length of transition from marriage to parenthood has been considerably shortened during the past four decades. A recent study (Wang Peng and Yang Quanhe, 1996), while highlighting the phenomenon that the shortening of the first birth interval during the 16-year period 1970-1985 had occurred concurrently with a rise in mean female age at first marriage (figure 7), suggests that the substantial narrowing in the first birth interval is largely due to increasing sexual activity among young couples. While the government's advocacy of late marriage has to some extent precipitated couple's childbearing after

Figure 7. Mean female age at first marriage and mean length of the first birth interval: 1970-1985

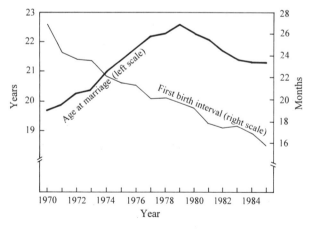

Source: **Wang Peng and Yang Quanhe,** "Age at marriage and the first birth interval: the emerging change in sexual behaviour among young couples in China", *Population and Development Review,* vol. 22, No. 2, 1996.

marriage, the study argued that the reduction in the first birth interval was not simply a compensating behaviour for late marriage, but had largely been brought about by increased coital frequency among the young, both married and unmarried.

The changes that have occurred in the sexual behaviour of young couples have been attributed by Wang Peng and Yang Quanhe to several aspects of the social changes that had swept the country since the founding of the People's Republic, particularly "a fundamental transformation in the marriage system; a massive expansion in formal education and non-familial employment, both largely supported by the socialist state; and a significant change in young couple's sexual behaviour, unintentionally assisted by the government family planning programme that widely disseminated information on matters of sexuality and reproduction".

Under the traditional system of arranged marriages, the groom and bride would, by and large, meet each other for the first time on the day of the wedding ceremony, and would thus start their marital life as total strangers. The newly-weds are also usually admonished by the groom's mother to observe moderation in sexual activities to avoid depletion of the male's strength or vitality. Young couples also had to avoid intimacy and physical contact in front of family members or in public. It was also customary for the new bride to return to her natal home for periods extending from several months to a year to spend time with her parents and siblings. On account of these factors and constraints, coital frequency was low, resulting in long first birth intervals. On the other hand, the decisive shift towards love marriages, or marriages contracted on their own by the couple, has been accompanied by increased attraction and intimacy between bride and groom at the time of marriage, leading to increased coital frequency and shortening of first birth intervals.

The rapid expansion in education and in employment outside the households has resulted in increased opportunities for young people to meet face to face, fall in love, and marry of their own free will. Compared with rural areas, the newly-weds in urban areas are also more likely to set up their own households and live separately from the groom's parents. Such relationships and arrangements are conducive to greater intimacy between the groom and the bride. Analysis of available data also shows that women's high educational attainment is associated with short first birth intervals.

There have also been rapid changes in the norms regarding sexuality since the opening of China to the outside world and the gradual withdrawal of the government from the private lives of citizens. With increased exposure of young people to matters related to sexuality through popular literature and other media, discussions regarding sex and sexuality have become more open and sexuality has come to be treated more as a source of individual pleasure and satisfaction and less as a matter of reproduction. Further, in spreading knowledge about contraception, the family planning programme has also helped to disseminate information about sex and reproduction widely. In fact, the most rapid narrowing in the first birth interval coincided with the spread of the family planning programmes in the 1970s.

Over the years there have also been changes in the fertility rates of Chinese women at all ages within the reproductive span, and these changes have been more marked in respect of women in the youngest and older age groups. Estimates based on the data from the 1982 One-per-Thousand Fertility Sampling Survey and data from the censuses of 1982 and 1990 indicate that, between 1953 and 1981, the fertility rate dropped by about 94 per cent for women in the 15-59 age group, by about 86 per cent for those aged 40-44 years, and by about 83 per cent for women aged 35-39 years. Throughout this 28-year period, the highest fertility rates have been for women aged 25-29 years, and these dropped by only about 18 per cent between 1953 and 1981. However, between 1981 and 1989, the fertility of young women aged 15-19 years increased by about 267 per cent and that of women aged 20-24 by about 38 per cent, while the rates for women in the higher age groups had declined. In 1989, the highest fertility rate was experienced by women aged 20-24 years (table 49).

Table 49. Age-specific fertility rates in selected years: 1953-1989

Age	1953	1964	1981	1989
15-19	0.096	0.070	0.006	0.022
20-24	0.275	0.296	0.144	0.199
25-29	0.286	0.309	0.235	0.156
30-34	0.242	0.261	0.085	0.056
35-39	0.192	0.193	0.032	0.020
40-44	0.102	0.096	0.014	0.006
45-49	0.016	0.011	0.003	0.002
Total fertility rate	6.05	6.18	2.61	2.29

Source: The 1953 and 1964 data are estimates based on the 1982 One-per-Thousand Fertility Sampling Survey, and the 1981 and 1989 data are estimates derived from the data of the 1982 and 1990 population censuses respectively.

Although there has been a drastic reduction in the number of children born to the average Chinese woman during the past four decades, this decline has been uneven across the various administrative divisions of the country. In mega cities such as Shanghai and Beijing, as well as in parts of highly urbanized provinces like Jilin and Heilongjiang, where the one-child policy and family planning programmes are vigorously implemented and the desire for small family size is strong, the average number of children per woman has declined to below replacement level. But on the average, women still have more than two children in the rural areas of most provinces, and three to four children in Henan, Tibet, Xinjiang and Guizhou, which are populated mostly by ethnic minorities (annex table D.3). Nevertheless, the changes that have occurred in the reproductive behaviour of Chinese women in recent decades is remarkable for a country with one fifth of the world population and a relatively low level of development.

It is also relevant to note that in China, as in most other countries, the sexual behaviour of unmarried people is very rarely taken into consideration in surveys and research studies, and hence there is very little information relating to premarital sexual activities and unwanted pregnancies. For various reasons, never-married women have not been covered in the several official fertility surveys conducted in the country from time to time. However, small-scale studies limited to particular areas provide direct evidence

55

that sexual activity among unmarried people is becoming increasingly common.

In their recent study, Wang Peng and Yang Quanhe concluded that although the conditional probability of premarital conception is low in China, there was evidence of an increasing trend over time and that in the mid-1980s, 5 out of every 100 pregnancies were conceived before marriage. Perhaps, the most incontrovertible evidence regarding the occurrence of premarital sex is the incidence of induced abortion among unmarried women; various studies indicate that a substantial proportion of all abortions in the country occur among unmarried women.

In view of the increasing opportunities for education and the increasing age at marriage, the number of never-married persons is bound to increase in the future. Available evidence indicates that over 90 per cent of the never married are under 30 years of age. The increase in the interval between menarche and marriage also means that an increasing number of young people will engage in premarital sex and will be exposed to the risk of unwanted pregnancy for a long period. Given the increasing incidence of premarital sexual activity, it becomes necessary to include never-married women in a meaningful way in national fertility and health surveys so as to obtain comprehensive information regarding the sexual and fertility behaviour of all women of reproductive age.

It also has to be mentioned that in China, some segments of the population are beyond the reach of the country's one-child policy and family planning programmes. The first decade of the reforms after 1979 saw the movement around the country of more than 50 million people, and in recent years an estimated 80 million rural Chinese have left their homes and farms to take transient wage-earning jobs, mostly in the booming cities. Couples of childbearing age account for a large percentage of this floating population, and the percentage of this population who are married women of reproductive age is estimated at 37 per cent, double the proportion among permanent residents. These couples or their families take advantage of the lack of permanent address to evade birth quotas

and unwanted visits from zealous population control cadres. Most migrant families have more than two children each and recent official reports point to a high incidence of unexpected pregnancies and births among them. However, the government has recently established a network to monitor the reproductive health services for the floating couples at childbearing age, and is encouraging the receiving neighbourhoods to take responsibility for delivering family planning services to the floating population.

(c) Marital disruption

Disruption in married life occurs as a result of divorce/separation or widowhood. While the proportion of the population living in a state of marital disruption is important from the demographic point of view, marital disruption also seriously affects family life.

(i) Divorce/separation

In the semi-colonial and semi-feudal China of the past, where socio-cultural values and legal codes were largely influenced by Confucian ideals, a wife had no right to demand divorce from her husband, but the husband could forsake his wife for any one of seven legally recognized reasons: her adultery, jealousy, contraction of a loathsome disease, garrulity, disobedience to his parents, failure to bear children, or theft committed by her. These grounds might not be invoked if the family, having been poor, had become wealthy during the marriage, or if the wife had observed mourning for her parents-in-law, or if she had no family of her own to which she could return. However, the incidence of divorce is reported to have been very rare in those days.

Since the founding of the People's Republic, the old order has been changing yielding place to new. The importance attached to the protection of marriage and the family, and the commitment to ensuring equality of men and women in the family as well as in other aspects led to the enactment of the 1950 Marriage Law. Among others, this Law recognized divorce by mutual consent, which, like other forms of divorce, had to be registered with the local government. *Ex parte* divorce could be granted by the county or municipal governments, though only after mediation both at that level and at district level had failed. The husband was not permitted to apply for divorce when the wife was pregnant or for a year after the birth. *Ex parte* divorce was also not granted to the spouse of a member of the armed forces still in touch with his/her family. If after divorce, one party runs into economic difficulty, it is the duty of the other spouse to render economic assistance.

Over the years, people's attitudes towards divorce and separation have changed considerably; by and large, divorce and separation have come to be regarded as socially undesirable. Most families, in both rural and urban areas, continue to preserve the traditional morality intact. As noted in the previous section, only about 0.6 per cent of all persons aged 15 years and over were reported to be divorced at the 1990 census, the proportion for females being half that for males (table 15).

(ii) Widowhood

The incidence of widowhood is a function of mortality, and since risks of death increase with advancing age, the incidence of widowhood also increases with increasing age. But the proportion of persons reported as being widowed is also partially dependent on social customs and values governing the remarriage of widowed persons.

According to the 1990 census, about 6 per cent of all persons aged 15 years and over were reported to be widowed, the proportion among women (8.5 per cent) being more than double that of 3.8 per cent recorded for men (table 15). The higher incidence of widowhood among women is due to a combination of several factors. In China, as in most Asian countries, women marry men who are a few years senior to them in age, and the higher mortality rates for men, particularly in the older age groups, means that generally husbands will die before the wives. Further, despite the fact that family laws of the country prohibit any interference with the remarriage of widows, a widowed male still has better chances of remarriage than a widowed female. Studies indicate that young men are reluctant to marry a widow.

E. WOMEN IN ECONOMIC LIFE

1. Historical scenario

Available studies indicate that in traditional China, women's participation in directly remunerative work was minor since they were mostly engaged in domestic chores. The household work, which was the exclusive responsibility of women and which was indispensable to the family's well-being, was demanding and often arduous. It was the woman's task to prepare meals for family members, and this task involved, in addition to cooking, gathering fuel, drawing and fetching water, husking and grinding or polishing grains, and preserving surplus vegetables and fruits. In many households, women were also engaged in making bean curd and fermented alcoholic drinks, preparing tobacco leaves for smoking, stitching clothes etc.

The role played by women in agricultural production varied across the regions as well as social classes. While they played a significant role in agriculture in certain rice-producing areas of the south, it was exceptional for women to perform farm work in some villages in the north. According to random surveys conducted in the early 1930s, men contributed to about 80 per cent of the farm labour, women 13 per cent and children 7 per cent, but these proportions varied from one region to another. Women performed around 16 per cent of farm work in the rice-growing areas as a whole as against only about 9 per cent in the wheat region.

Generally speaking, women worked more on the farm than men in sparsely populated regions characterized by a system of shifting cultivation, while men did much more farm work than women in densely populated regions, where extensive plough cultivation had to be practised. However, in regions of intensive cultivation of irrigated land, both men and women had to work hard in order to support the family on a small plot of land. Further, while women did more farm work in the south than in the north, their role in agricultural production was relatively minor in almost all localities. By and large, women's farm work was highly seasonal and also limited to such chores as harvesting and weeding. With the exception of a few places in the south, it also remained the ideal that women should not engage in agricultural work.

Besides the burdensome domestic chores, there were other factors that hindered women's participation in agricultural work. Although household work was arduous, farm work was still heavier, and in a situation where women were continuously pregnant, they were prevented from carrying heavy loads or even walking any distance. Second, since women had customarily not been doing any farm work, they lacked the necessary skills and techniques and were considered incapable of performing farm work in a satisfactory manner. Further, there were socio-cultural prejudices against women working outside the home, particularly if that meant being in the company of men.

Studies also indicate that in rural areas, subsidiary occupations such as tea-processing, hog- and poultry-raising, spinning, weaving, basket-making and other handicrafts accounted for a significant proportion, 14 per cent, of the family income. But women's contribution to these activities was again quite small, providing, on an average, only 16 per cent of the required labour, and varied from one region to another depending on the amount of occupied time devoted to farm activities. For instance, in the wheat-millet areas of the north, where women seldom participated in agriculture, they contributed about 25 per cent of the total labour involved in subsidiary occupations; the corresponding proportion was only 13 per cent in the rice-tea areas.

The government was quick to realize that women were oppressed because they were cut off from productive and directly remunerative work and therefore had to be economically dependent on men, and that it would not be possible to emancipate women as long as they were restricted to unpaid domestic chores. During the 1950s, considerable efforts were made and the necessary measures adopted to empower women economically and to induce them to work outside their homes.

In the semi-feudal China of the past, poor farmers and farm labourers, who together accounted for 70 per cent of the rural population, owned only 10 per cent of the land, and women had no right to own any land. Consequently, in the very early days of the People's Republic, widespread and profound land reform was implemented in accordance with the principle of distributing land on the basis of the number of members in a family. Thus, rural women were able to obtain land, just like their male counterparts, and become masters of their piece of soil. The 1992 Law on the Protection of the Rights and Interests of Women makes special provision for the use of land by women in rural areas. Women enjoy equal rights to those of men with regard to their share of the land, whether for purposes of house-building, subsistence farming or contract farming.

In the past, it was generally impossible for women to obtain credit facilities and loans in their individual capacity: they could do so only in their husbands' names. The necessary steps were therefore initiated to enable rural women to obtain credit facilities for agricultural production and other income-generating activities, and by the end of the 1980s, nearly two thirds of China's provinces had streamlined the procedures and provided easy facilities for women to obtain loans at preferential interest rates. For example, in Fujian Province alone, the agricultural banks provided rural women with loans totalling over 100 million yuan for agricultural production every year. In Heilongjiang Province, the Agricultural Bank provided 15 million yuan loans at a discount rate to encourage rural women to adopt improved methods of pig-raising. During the five-year period 1988-1993, agricultural banks at different levels provided rural women with more than 7 billion yuan in loans, which have enabled the women to purchase materials for the production and processing of agricultural products.

In order to overcome the dearth of skills among women, the Women's Association organized training classes which, besides imparting skills, also encouraged the women to take pride in the abilities they had once been ashamed to possess and also to overcome the obstacles in their way. Once the women were trained, demonstrations were organized to convince everybody that women could perform most agricultural jobs as well as men could. In 1989 and 1991, the All-China Women's Federation launched a learning and competing campaign in which husbands and wives not only learned to read, write and acquire working skills, but also competed with each other in achievements and contributions. These campaigns helped millions of women to participate more efficiently in economic activities.

Appropriate measures were also taken to overcome other obstacles that stood in the way of women working outside their homes. The socio-cultural prejudice against women engaging in farm work was most easily eliminated in those areas where there was an acute shortage of labour, often caused by the absence of men, who were away fighting in either the Civil War or the Korean War. In other areas, husbands and other family members were willing to permit women to work outside the home once they realized that women's earnings brought greater prosperity to the family. The conflict between domestic and outside work was resolved to a large extent by the exchange of labour; older women in the family assumed responsibility for cooking and looking after the children while the younger women and mothers were away at work. The gradual provision of creches and nurseries and the use of labour-saving consumer products also facilitated the participation of women in income-earning activities outside their homes.

The campaign to encourage women to participate actively and directly in economic production was closely linked to the transition from individual to collective farming. In collective agriculture, women seldom worked in the same team as men but were more often organized into special women's teams. This arrangement helped to reduce the suspicion or accusation that women who left home to work were looking for love affairs. Efforts were also made to allocate to women tasks that could be easily performed by them. Initially, there were complaints about discrimination against women in the matter of giving work points for job accomplishments, and there was agitation for equal pay for equal work. Consequently, laws were passed providing for the principle of equal pay for equal work for men and women.

On account of the concerted efforts made, more and more women in both rural and urban areas have been entering the workforce and have become economically self-supporting. Estimates indicate that about 70 per cent of rural women were engaged in agricultural work in 1957. In that year, the urban female labour force numbered 3.286 million, which was more than five times the number in 1949. Although the earnings of the husbands are still higher than those of the wife, her earnings often constitute a substantial proportion, about 40 per cent, of the family income. Partly because of the importance of women's earnings in enhancing family prosperity, husband-wife relationships have increasingly been developing on the basis of equality, mutual respect and affection. Sample investigations show that in over 58 per cent of urban and rural families, important matters are decided jointly by the husband and wife.

Although women's overall economic status has improved tremendously since the founding of the People's Republic, because of the lower educational attainment of women, job opportunities are more limited for women than for men, and women are underrepresented in many relatively desirable jobs. Moreover, there is concern that the dismantling of the commune system of the 1970s, in which women were paid members of the agricultural labour force, and its replacement by family-based agricultural production quotas or contracts whereby most rural women no longer have earnings in their own right, have led to a decrease in women's income and increased their economic dependence in what are generally male-headed households.

2. The employed population

(a) Database

Prior to the founding of the People's Republic, China lacked a well-developed system for the collection, analysis and publication of labour statistics. Since 1949, efforts have been made to gradually establish a labour and wages statistical system as part of the statistical departments at various levels of administration. The coverage of this system has, however, been limited to a few vital economic sectors such as manufacturing, construction, transport and communication, and trade and commerce. In 1952, an employment census was conducted in the urban and rural areas, and this census was followed by nationwide censuses on the entire working staff, wages, insurance etc. in 1955, 1956 and 1957. On the basis of these censuses, a system for reporting employment and wages on a regular basis was instituted in 1959, and the data processed by the statistical bureaux of provinces, municipalities and autonomous regions are published annually in a consolidated form by the State Statistical Bureau. These data, though not comprehensive in nature, provide a fairly accurate picture of the employment trends and patterns in the country.

However, more comprehensive data regarding sectoral affiliations, occupational categories and work status of the employed population by sex are provided by the 1982 and 1990 population censuses which have included an all-round enumeration of the employed population on a nationwide scale according to the Industrial Classification Standards for the National Economy, and the Occupational Classification Standards formulated for the census. For the purposes of the census, the employed population was defined as that part of the population which receives remuneration for work or has an income by running a business. Those conforming to this criterion were deemed employed regardless of whether they obtained their jobs on the recommendation of government labour departments, or by organizing themselves on a voluntary basis, or through other channels; and whether they worked in state enterprises or collectives or as individual workers. More specifically, the employed were either: (a) persons who had permanent jobs during the reference period, including those actually working as well those temporarily not working owing to illness or injury, those on vacation, those released temporarily from work for further schooling or training, and those prevented from working owing to bad weather, technical difficulties or temporary suspension of production; or (b) persons who, though without permanent occupa-

tions, were doing odd jobs on the date of the census and had engaged in socially productive labour for at least 16 days in the month.

(b) Employment levels and trends

Data from the censuses indicate that the total number of employed persons in China increased by about 125.7 million, or by about 24 per cent, between 1982 and 1990. During this period, while the number of employed males increased by 62.6 million, or 21.3 per cent, the number of employed females increased by 63.2 million, or 27.7 per cent. The percentage increase in total employed persons was much higher in the urban (45.6 per cent) than in the rural (18.1 per cent) areas, and in both these areas the increase was significantly higher for females than for males (table 50). Analysis not shown in the table also indicates that the proportion of employed females to the total number of females aged 15 years and over increased from 70.1 per cent in 1982 to 73 per cent in 1990, reflecting the increasing participation of women in economic activities over the years.

The larger increase in employed females compared with employed males could be attributed to a combination of several factors. In the first instance, the development of a market-oriented economy had provided a favourable environment for women to participate in work outside their homes, and consequently an increasing number of women who used to be doing only domestic chores have been entering the formal labour market. For example, of the 97.39 million women reported as not being employed in the 1982 census, 69.52 million, or 71.4 per cent, were engaged in household work. But in 1990, of the 107.53 million who were not classified as employed, only 62.62 million, or 58.2 per cent, were reported to be engaged in household chores. Thus, there has been a substantial reduction in the number of women performing household work as well as in their relative share in the total number of women reported as being not employed between 1982 and 1990.

Second, the greater increase in employed females has also been occasioned by a greater

Table 50. Growth and composition of the employed population by rural and urban area and by sex: 1982 and 1990 censuses

Area and sex	Employed persons (millions)		Increase (1982-1990)		Percentage composition	
	1982	1990	Number (millions)	Percentage	1982	1990
China: Both sexes	521.50	647.24	125.74	24.1	100.0	100.0
Male	293.66	356.23	62.57	21.3	56.3	55.0
Female	227.84	291.01	63.17	27.7	43.7	45.0
Urban: Both sexes	114.32	166.39	52.07	45.5	100.0	100.0
Male	65.90	94.77	28.87	43.8	57.6	57.0
Female	48.42	71.62	23.20	47.9	42.4	43.0
Rural: Both sexes	407.18	480.85	73.67	18.1	100.0	100.0
Male	227.76	261.46	33.70	14.8	55.9	54.4
Female	179.42	219.39	39.97	22.3	44.1	45.6

Source: 1982 and 1990 population censuses.

increase in the number of employed females in the rural than the urban areas. Between 1982 and 1990, the number of employed females increased overall by 63.17 million; of this increment, 39.97 million, or 63.3 per cent, was contributed by rural areas where, in addition to the introduction of the household contract responsibility system with remuneration linked to output, the structural changes in the rural economy provided the rural women with increasing opportunities for paid as well as self-employment in a large number of areas, such as farming, forestry, animal husbandry, fishing, manufacturing, commerce, transportation, construction and services. By the end of 1992, the rural non-agricultural enterprises are estimated to have employed more than 100 million people, of whom more than 40 million were women, largely engaged in the food, clothing, knitting, toy-making, electronics, traditional handicrafts and service industries. Today, women account for one third of the 14 million self-employed persons in rural areas.

The sex-differential growth rates resulted in significant changes in the sex composition of the employed population between 1982 and 1990. Overall, 43.7 per cent of the employed persons were female in 1982; this proportion had increased to 45.0 per cent in 1990. During the same period, the proportionate share of females in the total number of employed persons had increased from 42.4 to 43.0 per cent in urban areas, and from 44.1 to 45.6 per cent in

rural areas. In both 1982 and 1990, women constituted a higher proportion of the employed persons in rural than in urban areas (table 50).

Although, in 1990, women constituted 45 per cent of the country's employed population, this proportion had varied from one administrative division to another. It ranged from a low of 39 per cent in Heilongjiang and Shanxi provinces to between 40 and 43 per cent in Fujian, Jilin, Zhejiang and Liaoning provinces and Nei Mongol autonomous region and the municipalities of Beijing and Tianjin, to a high of over 47 per cent in Jiangxi, Yunnan and Guizhou provinces. In all other administrative divisions, the proportionate share of women in the total number of employed persons varied between 43 and 46 per cent (annex table E.1). These variations largely reflect the socio-cultural values relating to and opportunities for women's employment outside the homes in the respective areas.

The age-specific employment rates by sex given in table 51 indicate that between 1982 and 1990, there was a decline in these rates for both males and females at ages 15-24 and that this decline was more marked at ages 15-19, perhaps owing to increasing participation of youth in the education system. It will also be noted from table 51 that in 1982, as well as in 1990, the employment rate for females at ages 15-19 was about seven percentage points higher than the corresponding rate for males, reflecting

Table 51. Age-sex-specific employment rates: 1982 and 1992 censuses

(Percentage)

Age group	1982 census China		1990 census China		Urban		Rural	
	Male	Female	Male	Female	Male	Female	Male	Female
15-19	70.55	77.82	61.38	68.22	39.97	42.13	68.21	76.43
20-24	96.13	90.34	92.38	89.62	81.41	79.90	96.55	93.02
25-29	98.59	88.77	97.87	90.79	95.51	87.78	98.96	92.10
30-34	98.83	88.77	98.58	90.93	97.36	89.76	99.17	91.49
35-39	98.86	88.46	98.83	91.02	98.06	89.52	99.16	91.76
40-44	98.63	83.34	98.66	88.12	98.18	85.22	98.86	89.31
45-49	97.47	70.57	97.68	81.01	96.91	73.37	97.99	84.09
50-54	91.42	50.90	93.32	61.96	89.93	41.70	94.76	70.69
55-59	82.96	32.87	83.60	44.94	72.98	21.40	88.05	54.16
60-64	63.66	16.37	63.18	27.21	38.52	12.00	72.53	32.53
65+	31.11	4.73	32.59	7.95	18.96	3.58	37.02	9.33

Source: 1982 and 1990 population censuses.

the fact that more boys than girls at these ages continue their schooling, in keeping with the age-old family tradition favouring higher education for sons while daughters are detained at home to help in domestic chores. At ages 25 and above, despite substantial increases between 1982 and 1990, the female rates are significantly lower than the male rates, and this disparity is more pronounced at ages 50 and over. At each age group beyond 50 years, the 1990 male rates exceed the female rates by more than 30 percentage points, owing to the fact that women retire earlier than men (figure 8).

Figure 8. Age-sex-specific employment rates: 1982 and 1990 censuses

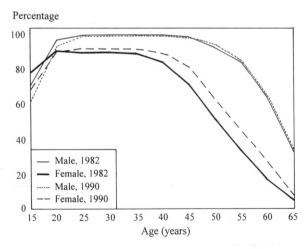

Source: "Population and development in China; facts and figures", *China Population Today*, vol. 11, No. 3, 1994, Special Issue for the International Conference on Population and Development, Cairo, 1994.

It is also evident from table 51 that in 1990, the age-specific employment rates for both males and females were higher in the rural than in the urban areas and the differential was more marked at ages 15-24 than at older age groups. For instance, at ages 15-19 years the rural male rate exceeded the urban male rate by 28.2 percentage points, while the rural female rate was 34.3 percentage points higher than the corresponding urban rate. Similarly, at ages 20-24, the rural male rate was 15 percentage points higher and the rural female rate 13 percentage points higher than the corresponding rates in urban areas. The higher rural employment percentage is due to two factors; the rural population has more or less immediate access to jobs without waiting for job assignments, as in urban areas; and in the rural areas a substantial number of persons in the 15-24 age group go to work instead of attending secondary schools or colleges. The urban-rural differential in age-specific employment rates was generally more pronounced or significant in the case of females than males.

3. Employment structure

Data from the 1982 and 1990 censuses show that there have been significant changes in the employment structure in terms of industrial or economic sectoral attachment, occupational distribution and educational background of the employed persons during this eight-year period.

(a) Industrial attachment

For purposes of classifying the employed persons according to the nature of economic activities performed by the enterprises and institutions in which they were engaged, the censuses used the Industrial Classification Standards for the National Economy which were adapted from the International Standard Industrial Classification of All Economic Activities formulated by the Statistical Office of the United Nations. The adaptation was considered necessary to ensure, among others things, that the standards accorded with what was required for the study of the national economy's overall balance and for differentiating material production from non-material production. The distribution of employed persons by industrial sector for 1982 and 1990 is shown in table 52.

It will be noted from table 52 that, between 1982 and 1990, there was an increase in the number of males and females employed in various industrial or economic sectors, except for a decrease in the number of males employed in the mining and quarrying and "other" sectors. In quantitative terms, the largest increase in employment occurred in the agricultural and allied industrial sectors, with the number of males employed in this sector increasing by 39.65 million, or 19.2 per cent, and the number of females employed increasing by 43.79 million, or 24.6 per cent. The second and third largest increases in the number employed took place in the manufacturing and commerce sectors respectively, where again the increases were greater in respect of females than males. With regard to the number of additional persons employed between 1982 and 1990, females also outnumbered males in the health and education sectors.

The sex-differentiated growth in employment in various sectors between 1982 and 1992 is also reflected in the changes in percentage distribution of employed males and females

Table 52. Distribution and growth of employed persons by major industrial sector and
sex: 1982 and 1990 censuses

Industrial sector	1982		1990		Increase 1982-1990			
					Male		Female	
	Male (10,000)	Female (10,000)	Male (10,000)	Female (10,000)	Number (10,000)	Percent-age	Number (10,000)	Percent-age
Agriculture, animal husbandry, forestry, fishing	20 650	17 765	24 615	22 144	3 965	19.2	4 379	24.6
Manufacturing	4 337	2 922	4 945	3 713	708	16.7	791	27.0
Mining and quarrying	64	18	60	20	−4	−6.3	2	11.1
Construction	893	208	976	188	83	9.3	−20	−9.6
Transport and communications	693	205	957	218	264	38.1	13	6.3
Commerce, catering trades etc.	880	671	1 372	1 205	492	55.9	534	79.6
Housing and public utilities management	135	109	342	277	207	160.7	168	154.1
Health	213	197	241	276	28	13.1	79	40.1
Education, culture and art	800	438	885	625	85	10.6	187	42.7
Scientific research and technical services	76	44	91	54	15	19.7	10	22.7
Finance and insurance	70	32	129	84	59	84.3	52	162.5
Government agencies	638	164	1 002	293	364	57.1	129	78.6
Others	18	11	8	4	−10	−55.6	−6	−54.5
All sectors	29 367	22 784	35 623	29 101	6 256	21.3	6 317	27.7

Source: 1982 and 1990 population censuses.

during this eight-year period. In 1982, as well as in 1990, the largest proportions among males and females were employed in the agricultural sector, followed by the manufacturing sector, but the proportions employed in these two major sectors declined during these eight years, with the combined proportion for females declining from 90.7 to 88.4 per cent, and that for males from 85.1 to 83.0 per cent. At the same time, there have been significant increases in the relative shares of women employed in several sectors: in agriculture from 46.2 to 47.4 per cent; in manufacturing from 40.3 to 44.4 per cent; in mining and quarrying from 22.0 to 25.0 per cent; in commerce and trade from 43.3 to 46.8 per cent; in the health sector from 46.6 to 53.4 per cent; in the education sector from 35.4 to 41.4 per cent; in scientific research from 36.7 to 39.4 per cent; in finance and insurance from 31.4 to 39.4 per cent; and in government agencies from 20.4 to 22.6 per cent. In the transport and communications and "other" sectors, there was a decline in the percentage share of women in the total number employed (table 53).

(b) Occupational category

The 1982 and 1990 population censuses classified the occupations or nature of work performed by the employed persons into eight major occupational categories. The occupational classification standards used in the censuses of China were adapted from the International Standard Classification of Occupations formulated by the United Nations International Labour Office, and renders possible the analysis of the employed persons in terms of their skills and their distribution in various trades. The classification of the employed persons as reported in the 1982 and 1990 censuses, by major occupational categories and sex, is shown in table 54.

It will be noted from table 54 that, between 1982 and 1990, the largest increase numerically was in respect of workers engaged in agricultural occupations, who also constituted the vast majority of employed persons in both census years. The number of female agricultural labourers increased by about 4.4 million, or

Table 53. Percentage distribution of employed persons by industrial sector and sex, and sex composition of employed persons by sex: 1982 and 1990 censuses

Industrial sector	Percentage distribution				Sex composition (%)			
	1982		1990		1982		1990	
	Male	Female	Male	Female	Male	Female	Male	Female
Agriculture, animal husbandry etc.	70.3	77.9	69.1	76.1	53.8	46.2	52.6	47.4
Manufacturing	14.8	12.8	13.9	12.3	49.7	40.3	55.6	44.4
Mining and quarrying	0.2	0.1	0.2	0.1	78.0	22.0	75.0	25.0
Construction	3.0	0.9	2.7	0.7	71.1	18.9	83.8	16.2
Transport and communications	2.4	0.9	2.7	0.8	77.2	22.8	81.6	18.4
Commerce, catering trades etc.	2.9	3.0	3.9	4.2	56.7	43.3	53.2	46.8
Housing and public utilities management	0.5	0.5	0.9	1.0	55.4	44.6	55.3	44.7
Health	0.7	0.9	0.7	1.0	52.0	48.0	46.6	53.4
Education, culture and art	2.7	1.9	2.5	2.2	64.6	35.4	48.6	41.4
Scientific research and technical services	0.2	0.2	0.2	0.2	63.3	36.7	61.6	38.4
Finance and insurance	0.2	0.2	0.4	0.3	68.6	31.4	60.6	39.4
Government agencies	2.1	0.7	2.8	1.0	79.6	20.4	77.4	22.6
Others	–	–	–	–	62.1	37.9	66.7	33.3
All sectors	100.0	100.0	100.0	100.0	56.3	43.7	55.0	45.0

Source: 1982 and 1990 population censuses.

64

Table 54. Distribution and growth of employed persons by broad occupational group and sex: 1982 and 1990 censuses

(Numbers in tens of thousands)

Occupational category	1982 Male	1982 Female	1990 Male	1990 Female	Increase 1982-1990 Male Number	Increase 1982-1990 Male Percentage	Increase 1982-1990 Female Number	Increase 1982-1990 Female Percentage
Professional and technical personnel	1 633	1 012	1 883	1 556	250	15.3	544	53.8
Leaders/managers of government offices, political party organizations, enterprises etc.[a]	729	84	1 002	130	273	37.5	46	54.8
Office workers and related personnel[b]	513	166	838	289	325	63.4	123	74.1
Commercial workers	510	432	1 039	909	529	103.7	477	110.4
Service workers	599	551	750	801	151	25.2	250	45.4
Labourers in agriculture, forestry, animal husbandry and fishery	19 972	17 566	23 781	21 901	3 809	19.1	4 355	19.0
Production and transport workers and related personnel	5 384	2 953	6 312	3 501	928	17.2	548	18.6
Workers not classified by occupation	27	20	18	14	−9	−33.3	−6	−30.0
All occupations	29 367	22 784	35 623	29 101	6 256	21.3	6 317	27.7

Source: 1982 and 1990 population censuses.

[a] Corresponds to administrative and managerial workers in the United Nations International Standard Classification of Occupations.
[b] Corresponds to clerical and related workers in the United Nations International Standard Classification of Occupations.

by about 25 per cent, compared with an increase of about 3.8 million, or by 19.1 per cent, for males. But the most dramatic increase has been in regard to commercial workers; the inter-censal percentage increase in this occupational category was 110.4 per cent for female workers and 103.7 per cent for male workers. The increase in office workers and related personnel (persons engaged in clerical and related occupations) was also very high, with the percentage increase among females (74.1 per cent) being significantly higher than that among males (63.4 per cent). There have also been very significant increases in the number of females engaged in professional and technical occupations, as well as in the category of leaders/managers of government offices, political parties, enterprises and institutions. Between 1982 and 1990, the total number of professional and technical personnel increased by 7.94 million, of whom 5.44 million, or 68.5 per cent, were females.

The relative share of the employed persons engaged in various occupations has also changed owing to differences in their rate of growth between 1982 and 1990. Among females, there

has been a decline in the proportion engaged as labourers in agriculture and allied occupations from 77.1 to 75.3 per cent, and as production and transport workers from 13.0 to 12.0 per cent, and a significant increase in the proportions engaged as professional and technical personnel and as office workers and related personnel. In 1990, women constituted a majority (51.6 per cent) only in the occupational category of service workers; in all other occupational categories, their proportionate share was less than that of men, being the lowest (11.5 per cent) in the higher-level occupational category of leaders/managers of government offices, mass and political party organizations, enterprises and institutions (table 55).

Although the proportionate share of women in the total number of employed persons had increased from 43.7 per cent in 1982 to 45.0 per cent in 1990, the majority of the women continue to work in the informal sector and their proportionate share of employment in the modern sector is rather low. Further, women are generally engaged in work which carries low pay and occupies a relatively lower status within various occupational categories. More

Table 55. Percentage distribution and sex composition of employed persons by major occupational category: 1982 and 1990 censuses

Occupational category	Percentage distribution				Sex composition (%)			
	1982		1990		1982		1990	
	Male	Female	Male	Female	Male	Female	Male	Female
Professional and technical personnel	5.6	4.5	5.3	5.4	61.7	38.3	54.8	45.2
Leaders/managers of government offices, political party organizations, enterprises etc.[a]	2.5	0.4	2.8	0.5	89.7	10.3	88.5	11.5
Office workers and related personnel[b]	1.8	0.7	2.4	1.0	75.6	24.4	74.4	25.6
Commercial workers	1.7	1.9	2.9	3.1	54.1	45.9	53.3	46.7
Service workers	2.1	2.4	2.1	2.7	52.1	47.9	48.4	51.6
Labourers in agriculture, forestry, animal husbandry and fishery	68.0	77.1	66.8	75.3	53.2	46.8	52.1	47.9
Production and transport workers and related personnel	18.3	13.0	17.7	12.0	64.6	35.4	64.3	35.7
Workers not classified by occupation	–	–	–	–	57.4	42.6	56.3	43.7
All occupations	100.0	100.0	100.0	100.0	56.3	43.7	55.0	45.0

Source: 1982 and 1990 population censuses.

[a] Corresponds to administrative and managerial workers in the United Nations International Standard Classification of Occupations.
[b] Corresponds to clerical and related workers in the United Nations International Standard Classification of Occupations.

than three fourths of employed females are engaged as labourers in agriculture, forestry, animal husbandry and fisheries. Even though women constitute about 45 per cent of all employed persons categorized as professional and technical personnel, they are largely engaged at the middle and lower levels as nurses and paramedics in the health sector, as teachers in the educational services, and at the technician and craftsman levels in the science and engineering occupations.

The principle of equal pay for equal work for men and women is in general practised in China, although some gaps in income still exist owing to current differences in educational and professional competence as well as occupational composition. In urban areas, women generally receive 77.4 per cent of the pay given to men, while in rural areas women's earnings average 81.4 per cent of the earnings of men.

(c) Educational background

An important reason why women are very much underrepresented at higher levels and more remunerative occupations is their relatively lower level of educational attainment compared with men. The percentage distribution of the employed persons in 1990 by level of educational attainment and sex given in table 56 more or less corresponds to that of the general population shown in table 35.

It is evident from table 56 that, for the country as a whole, nearly 63 per cent of the employed females as against 48 per cent of the employed males were either illiterate or had completed only primary-level education. The proportion of employed persons with junior middle or senior middle school education was 49 per cent for males and 36 per cent for females. According to the 1990 census data, the overall educational attainment of employed females was much higher in urban than in rural areas. In the rural areas, nearly three fourths (73.5 per cent) of the employed females were either illiterate or had only primary-level education, compared with 30 per cent in the urban areas. While 65.4 per cent of the urban employed females had acquired junior middle or senior middle level education, only about 26 per cent of the rural employed females had done so.

In order to qualify women for a greater array of occupations and positions, the government has been attempting to enhance the

Table 56. Numerical and percentage distribution of employed persons by level of educational attainment, sex and urban-rural residence: 1990

(Numbers in tens of thousands)

Level of educational attainment	China				Urban				Rural			
	Male		Female		Male		Female		Male		Female	
	Number	%	Number	%	Number	%	Number	%	Number	%	Number	%
Illiterate and semi-illiterate	3 985	11.2	6 963	23.9	408	4.3	604	8.4	3 577	13.7	6 359	29.0
Primary school	13 166	37.0	11 317	38.9	2 057	21.7	1 547	21.6	11 110	42.5	9 770	44.5
Junior middle school	13 136	36.8	7 778	26.7	3 927	41.4	2 821	39.4	9 208	35.2	4 957	22.6
Senior middle school	4 475	12.6	2 692	9.3	2 323	24.5	1 859	26.0	2 152	8.2	833	3.8
Higher and tertiary	861	2.4	351	1.2	763	8.1	331	4.6	99	0.4	20	0.1
Total	35 623	100.0	29 101	100.0	9 477	100.0	7 162	100.0	26 146	100.0	21 939	100.0

Source: 1990 population census.

educational and professional level of women by establishing women's professional schools, women's cadre schools, and spare-time women's schools throughout the country. To meet the challenges for women's employment, China plans to readjust the industrial structure, increase job opportunities for women and gradually reduce the number of unemployed women in urban areas, so as to bring about equality in employment opportunities for men and women.

F. WOMEN IN PUBLIC LIFE

1. Background

As noted earlier, in the introduction to this profile, during the semi-colonial and semi-feudal era of the past, women in China had no political rights and were virtually excluded from participating in the country's public and political life. Nevertheless, over the past 100 years or so, Chinese women have waged dauntless struggles for their emancipation, and the 1911 Revolution, in particular, kindled a feminist movement which focused on equal rights for men and women and on the participation of women in public and political affairs. However, it was not until the birth of the Chinese Communist Party in 1921 that Chinese women were able to make any headway in regard to enhancing their socio-economic status and establishing themselves on an equal footing with their male counterparts.

Under the leadership of the Party, women, especially those employed in industry and agriculture, were mobilized and organized to form a broad united front, and in the Communist Party-led areas, the revolutionary powers issued a series of decrees and regulations to ensure the rights of women and improve their well-being.

The founding of the People's Republic accelerated the processes related to the emancipation of Chinese women. At the first Plenary Session of the Chinese People's Political Consultative Conference held in Beijing in 1949, there were 69 women delegates, accounting for 10.4 per cent of the delegates, representing women from various parts of the country. The Conference adopted the Common Programme, which was in the nature of a provisional constitution and which solemnly declared the toppling of the feudal system that had hitherto fettered women, and stated that women enjoyed equal rights with men in political, economic, cultural and educational fields and in other aspects of social life.

2. Women in politics

The Chinese Constitution, in article 34, states: "All citizens of the People's Republic of China who have reached the age of 18 have the right to vote and stand for election regardless of nationality, race, sex, occupation, family background, religious belief, education, property status or length of residence, excepting persons deprived of political rights according to the law". The Electoral Law of the People's Republic of China, promulgated in 1953, clearly stipulates that women enjoy the same rights as men to vote and to stand for election. The 1992 Law on the Protection of the Rights and Interests of Women stipulates that deputies to the National People's Congress (NPC) and local people's congresses at various levels should include an appropriate number of women, and that the proportion should be increased gradually. Consequently, in contemporary China, the majority of women concern themselves with national affairs; they are no longer apathetic, as was the case in China of the past. As a socialist country, China has involved the majority of its men and women in various types of political activities such as meetings, discussions, demonstrations and elections.

Since the 1950s, Chinese women have played an increasingly important role in the management of state and social affairs and have contributed substantially to the development of democracy and the building of the national legal system. For example, the National People's Congress, the highest organ of state power in China, is composed of deputies elected by the provinces, autonomous regions and municipalities under the control of the central government, and the armed forces. The deputies include representatives from various democratic parties, people's organizations, various nationalities, and

different classes and strata of society. When the first Congress was held in 1954, there were only 147 women deputies, accounting for about 12 per cent of all deputies. Since then, the number of women deputies has increased, with some fluctuations, and at the Eighth Congress held in 1993 there were 626 women deputies, constituting about 21 per cent of the total deputies. Similarly, the number of women in the Standing Committee (the permanent body of NPC) had increased from 4 in 1954 to 17 in 1993, or an increase from 5.0 per cent of total members to 12.7 per cent during the 39-year period (table 57).

Available data also indicate that women had accounted for about 11 per cent of all deputies elected by ethnic minorities until 1988, and that in 1993 there were 106 ethnic minority female deputies, accounting for about 17 per cent of all women deputies in that year. Three of these minority women were appointed to the Standing Committee. In 1993, nearly 95 per cent of eligible women cast their votes during elections for people's congresses at the local level, and the number of female deputies elected at the grass-roots levels accounted for 17 per cent of the total number of deputies; this percentage is higher than at the earlier congresses.

Women deputies to NPC participate actively in policy-making and legislative processes. They

Table 57. Female representatives in the National People's Congress and its Standing Committee: 1954-1993

| Congress session | National People's Congress | | | Standing Committee | |
| | Number of members | | | | |
	Total	Female	Percentage female	Number of female members	Percentage female
First (1954)	1 226	147	12.0	4	5.0
Second (1959)	1 226	150	12.2	5	6.3
Third (1964)	3 040	542	17.8	20	17.4
Fourth (1975)	2 885	653	22.6	42	25.1
Fifth (1978)	3 497	742	21.2	33	21.0
Sixth (1983)	2 978	632	21.2	14	9.0
Seventh (1988)	2 978	634	21.3	16	11.6
Eighth (1993)	2 978	626	21.0	19	12.7

Source: Stanley Rosen, "Women and political participation in China", *Pacific Affairs*, vol. 68, No. 3, 1995.

visit grass-roots-level units for fact-finding, inspection and listening to the opinions and views of the citizens. Based on such first-hand knowledge and information, women deputies have proposed several bills to improve the activities of the government and safeguard the rights and interests of women. For example, the Regulations on Labour Protection for Women Workers was promulgated by the State Council on the initiative of women deputies. Similarly, women deputies to people's congresses at various levels have played an important role in legislative work and in administration and social affairs. They are concerned mostly with problems in the areas of education, public health, environmental protection, protection of the rights and interests of women, children and the disabled, social security etc. The Law on the Protection of the Rights and Interests of Women was enacted on the basis of proposals submitted by women deputies and with their participation.

Another important decision-making organ is the Chinese People's Political Consultative Committee (CPPCC), which is an organization of the Patriotic United Front of the Chinese People. Chinese women take an important part in the activities of CPPCC at various levels. At the Eighth National Committee of CPPCC held in 1993, women accounted for 283, or 13.5 per cent, of the total membership, and 29 or 9.2 per cent of the Standing Committee members. Women members of CPPCC are outstanding persons from various walks of life, thus providing representation of a wide range of interests.

The Chinese Communist Party, the vanguard of the Chinese working class, has at present over 7 million women members, accounting for 14 per cent of the general membership. Many outstanding women work in various leading positions within the Party. The number of women members and alternate members in the Central Committee of the Party has increased from 8 at the Eighth Committee in 1956 to 24 at the current Fourteenth Committee (table 58).

The system of multi-party cooperation and political consultation under the leadership of the Communist Party of China forms the basic political system of the country. In 1989, the eight democratic parties had a total membership of 336,704, of whom 75,858, or 22.5 per cent, were women. The proportion of female members in the total membership also varied, from a low of 2.5 per cent in the September Third Study Society to a high of 39.7 per cent in the China Public Interest Party. The relative share of women in the membership of the central committees of the democratic parties also ranged from 6 to about 16 per cent (table 59). By the end of 1993, the eight parties together had 110,000 women members, of whom 203 were serving on the central committees.

At present, women serve in the party and government leading bodies in 23 of the 30 provinces, autonomous regions and municipalities; in 244 prefectures (cities, autonomous prefecture and leagues); and in 2,106 counties (districts and banners). This is a general improvement

Table 58. Female members in the Central Committee of the Chinese Communist Party: 1956-1992

Date of Central Committee	Members			Alternate members		
	All members	Female members	Percentage female	All members	Female members	Percentage female
Eighth (1956)	97	4	4.1	73	4	5.5
Ninth (1969)	170	13	7.6	109	10	9.2
Tenth (1973)	195	20	10.3	124	21	16.9
Eleventh (1977)	201	14	7.0	132	24	18.2
Twelfth (1982)	210	11	5.2	138	13	9.4
Thirteenth (1987)	175	10	5.7	110	12	10.9
Fourteenth (1992)	189	12	6.3	130	12	9.2

Source: Stanley Rosen, "Women and political participation in China", *Pacific Affairs*, vol. 68, No. 3, 1995.

Table 59. Female members in China's democratic parties: 1989

Democratic party	Party membership			Central Committee membership		
	All members	Female members	Percentage female	All members	Female members	Percentage female
Guomindang Revolutionary Committee	39 133	8 632	22.1	237	42	17.7
China Democratic League	99 092	26 709	27.0	299	39	13.0
China Association for Promoting Democracy	46 061	17 610	38.2	173	26	15.0
Chinese Peasants and Workers Democratic Party	44 813	7 879	17.6	158	24	15.2
China Public Interest Party	10 223	4 061	39.7	89	14	15.7
September Third Study Society	45 276	1 139	2.5	201	27	13.4
Taiwan Democratic League	1 160	407	35.1	49	3	6.1
China National Construction Association	50 946	9 421	18.5	170	13	7.6
All parties	336 704	75 858	22.5	1 376	188	13.7

Source: Stanley Rosen, "Women and political participation in China", *Pacific Affairs*, vol. 68, No. 3, 1995.

compared with the situation in 1985. In 517 cities throughout the country, 308 women assumed the position of mayor and vice-mayor in 1993.

Despite the progress achieved, the participation of women in political activities is still very low in China. While government policies strongly advocate equality between men and women in regard to participation in national- and local-level politics, there appears to be continued resistance to the increased and active involvement of women in political and other related activities. By and large, only a small proportion of women are engaged in political affairs and the number appointed to high-level key positions in the Party hierarchy is still very small.

Available information indicates that at the basic levels of county, township and small town, only about one per cent of top leaders of Party and government leading groups are women. Besides, women constitute a mere 3.8 per cent of the heads or deputy heads of townships or small towns, 5.9 per cent of all county chiefs or deputy chiefs, 5.8 per cent of all mayors and deputy mayors, and 6.5 per cent of all provincial governors or deputy governors. At the next higher level of provinces, autonomous regions and directly administered cities, the top leaders of the Party and government lead-

ing groups are all men; only five women have been appointed as deputy party secretaries at the provincial, prefectural or municipal levels.

As noted earlier, the substantial majority of political party members as well as of party decision-making and executive organs are still men. In fact, as will be noted from table 57, there has actually been a decline in the number of females and in their relative proportions among the representatives and standing committee members of the National People's Congress since 1978. Similarly, the number of women in the Central Committee of the Communist Party in 1992 was less than that in 1977 (table 58).

Several studies have also highlighted the fact the large majority of women participating in political activities at the national as well as local levels are engaged in work related to women's problems and issues, and very few are involved in matters relating to overall development. For instance, an analysis of the major positions of the 12 female full members of the 1992 Central Committee shows that four of these members are important leaders and another two have previously held leading positions in the Women's Federation (WF). It would appear that women who are leaders have at some point in their careers been mobilized to do women's work regardless of their own area of specialization.

Studies have also confirmed that at the grass-roots levels, a large majority of women involved in politics are doing women's work. For example, according to a 1992 survey of 21 townships and small towns in a county in Hunan Province, practically all office-bearers held the position of "cadre of WF"; only a small number of women cadres were from the staff of the family planning office and there were hardly any women in other official posts.

While the pronounced percentage of women in politics engaged in women's work may be considered as reflecting the importance that the Party accords to women's issues, the fact of the matter is that by and large such women cadres are restricted to doing only women's work and are not involved in other areas or aspects of overall development. Studies also point out that the inexperience of most women in areas outside traditional women's work has largely been responsible for their defeat when forced to run against their male counterparts for important hierarchical positions.

Traditional prejudice against women is also a factor still inhibiting the increased participation of women in political activities in China. In the countryside and in the remote areas, there are still many husbands who do not like their wives to be involved in political activities. Besides, female political activists must confront more rigorous trials, such as rumours and slander, jealousy and retaliation, stemming from gender prejudice. In general, young women show more interest in politics than older women, and generally female intellectuals have involved themselves in politics more deeply than female workers and peasants. Women in cities have taken part in politics more actively than women in towns and the countryside.

In order to further promote women's participation in governmental and political affairs, the government had adopted a series of measures in 1993. These include the formulation of programmes on training and selecting women cadres; it was required that by the end of 1995, all counties and 50 per cent of towns and villages should have at least one woman cadre in the leadership. Second, the training of women cadres was intensified, and since 1985 the national institutes for the training of middle- and high-level cadres have had a certain percentage of women students in every enrolment. Third, the government also stipulated a minimum proportion of political participation by women; for example, the Standing Committee of NPC had proposed that the proportion of women deputies at all levels should be above 20 per cent and should be increased gradually at every level.

3. Women in public administration

Over the years, there has been an increase in the number of women holding leading positions in government departments. For example, the number of women ministers and vice-ministers increased from 11 in 1985 to 18 in 1993; this represents an increase in the proportionate share of women from 5.2 to 6.6 per cent during this eight-year period. Currently, the ministers in charge of chemical industries, foreign trade and economic cooperation, and of the State Family Planning Commission, are women.

Available data also indicate that the number of women employed by various ministries and commissions under the State Council rose from 10.04 million, or 31.2 per cent of the total, in 1991 to 12.371 million, or 32.5 per cent of the total, in 1994. Among those occupying high-level positions in 1994, there were 18 women provincial vice-governors, and more than 300 women mayors or vice-mayors.

Women play an important role in strengthening the legal system and safeguarding the freedom and security of the people. China's judicial system has a large number of women: in 1992, there were 21,012 female judges and 4,512 female lawyers.

PART II
ANNEX TABLES

Table B.1 Numerical distribution of the enumerated population by five-year age group and sex: censuses of 1953, 1964, 1982 and 1990

Age group	1953		1964		1982		1990	
	Male	Female	Male	Female	Male	Female	Male	Female
0-4	46 104 886	43 170 240	51 461 891	48 680 065	48 983 813	45 720 548	61 049 130	55 389 289
5-9	33 264 941	29 510 596	49 283 349	44 894 085	57 026 296	53 709 575	51 630 875	47 705 868
10-14	29 082 491	24 707 743	45 005 259	41 346 386	67 837 932	63 973 025	50 183 593	47 043 099
15-19	27 072 984	24 653 803	32 356 349	29 759 139	63 804 581	61 561 763	61 650 589	58 507 832
20-24	23 718 199	22 606 396	26 483 045	24 337 706	37 880 114	36 482 906	64 233 023	61 528 151
25-29	21 711 735	20 604 268	26 798 450	23 596 958	47 746 258	44 817 624	53 512 983	50 754 542
30-34	19 595 040	18 491 570	24 719 798	21 986 292	37 930 244	35 027 993	43 706 133	40 169 574
35-39	18 778 517	17 502 857	21 591 224	19 578 688	28 565 678	25 655 951	44 568 847	41 782 965
40-44	16 454 333	15 200 608	18 438 348	17 206 867	25 827 570	22 610 373	33 335 977	30 371 687
45-49	14 676 352	14 084 045	15 710 681	15 142 155	25 073 117	22 330 214	25 855 900	23 232 041
50-54	12 435 470	11 921 207	13 292 133	13 213 249	21 528 986	19 286 515	24 110 355	21 509 204
55-59	10 398 207	10 161 827	10 749 195	11 819 052	17 493 925	16 400 402	21 839 937	19 869 398
60-64	8 006 104	8 494 082	8 125 730	9 545 724	13 709 397	13 652 807	17 481 948	16 494 306
65-69	5 400 767	6 374 478	5 109 214	6 525 902	10 171 973	11 088 397	12 917 485	13 415 035
70-74	3 308 199	4 507 616	3 002 343	4 375 906	6 434 731	7 913 314	8 344 204	9 706 376
75-79	1 368 411	2 224 077	1 377 689	2 379 677	3 496 703	5 120 340	4 689 104	6 244 820
80-84	473 106	955 331	461 892	977 293	1 350 776	2 353 829	1 993 954	3 358 736
85+	120 065	306 207	104 739	268 679	415 048	930 439	716 370	1 607 308
Unknown	–	–	2 445 682	2 430 925	363	407	–	–
All ages	291 969 807	275 476 951	356 517 011	338 064 748	515 277 505	488 636 422	581 820 407	548 690 231

Source: Yao Xinwu and Yin Hua, *Basic Data of China's Population*, Data User Service Series No. 1 (China Population Publishing House).

Table B.2 Percentage distribution of the enumerated population by five-year age group and sex: censuses of 1953, 1964, 1982 and 1990

Age group	1953			1964			1982			1990		
	Both sexes	Male	Female	Both sexes	Male	Female	Both sexes	Male	Female	Both sexes	Male	Female
0-4	15.74	15.79	15.67	14.42	14.43	14.40	9.44	9.51	9.36	10.30	10.49	10.10
5-9	11.06	11.39	10.71	13.56	13.82	13.28	11.03	11.07	10.99	8.79	8.87	8.69
10-14	9.48	9.96	8.97	12.43	12.62	12.23	13.13	13.17	13.09	8.60	8.63	8.57
15-19	9.12	9.27	8.95	8.94	9.08	8.80	12.49	12.38	12.60	10.63	10.60	10.66
20-24	8.16	8.12	8.21	7.32	7.43	7.20	7.40	7.35	7.47	11.12	11.04	11.21
25-29	7.46	7.44	7.48	7.26	7.52	6.98	9.22	9.27	9.17	9.22	9.20	9.25
30-34	6.71	6.71	6.71	6.72	6.93	6.50	7.27	7.36	7.17	7.42	7.51	7.32
35-39	6.39	6.43	6.35	5.93	6.06	5.79	5.40	5.54	5.25	7.64	7.66	7.62
40-44	5.58	5.62	5.52	5.13	5.17	5.09	4.82	5.01	4.63	5.64	5.73	5.54
45-49	5.07	5.03	5.11	4.44	4.41	4.48	4.72	4.87	4.57	4.34	4.44	4.23
50-54	4.29	4.26	4.33	3.82	3.73	3.91	4.07	4.18	3.95	4.04	4.14	3.92
55-59	3.62	3.56	3.69	3.25	3.02	3.50	3.38	3.40	3.36	3.69	3.75	3.62
60-64	2.91	2.74	3.08	2.54	2.28	2.82	2.73	2.66	2.78	3.01	3.00	3.01
65-69	2.08	1.85	2.31	1.68	1.43	1.93	2.12	1.97	2.27	2.33	2.22	2.44
70-74	1.38	1.13	1.64	1.06	0.84	1.29	1.43	1.25	1.62	1.60	1.43	1.77
75+	0.96	0.68	1.27	1.51	1.23	1.79	1.36	1.02	1.72	1.64	1.28	2.04
All ages	100.00	100.00	100.00	100.00	100.00	100.00	100.00	100.00	100.00	100.00	100.00	100.00

Source: Yao Xinwu and Yin Hua, *Basic Data of China's Population*, Data User Service Series No. 1 (China Population Publishing House).

Table B.3 Numerical and percentage distribution of the enumerated population by urban and rural residence: censuses of 1953, 1964, 1982 and 1990

Year	China		Urban		Rural	
	Number	Percentage	Number	Percentage	Number	Percentage
1953	582 603 417	100.00	77 257 282	13.26	505 346 135	86.74
1964	694 581 759	100.00	97 908 303	14.10	596 673 456	85.90
1982	1 003 913 927	100.00	206 309 144	20.55	797 604 783	79.45
1990	1 130 510 638	100.00	296 145 180	26.20	834 365 458	73.80

Source: Yao Xinwu and Yin Hua, *Basic Data of China's Population*, Data User Service Series No. 1 (China Population Publishing House).

Table C.1 Distribution of the enumerated population by urban and rural residence and sex: censuses of 1982 and 1990

Year	Urban areas			Rural areas		
	Both sexes	Male	Female	Both sexes	Male	Female
1982	206 309 144	108 020 720	98 288 424	797 604 783	407 256 785	390 347 998
1990	296 145 180	154 178 452	141 966 728	834 365 458	427 641 955	406 723 503

Source: Yao Xinwu and Yin Hua, *Basic Data of China's Population*, Data User Service Series No. 1 (China Population Publishing House).

Table C.2 Numerical distribution of the enumerated population by administrative region and sex: censuses of 1953, 1964, 1982 and 1990

Adiministrative region	1953		1964		1982		1990	
	Male	Female	Male	Female	Male	Female	Male	Female
Provinces								
Sichuan	32 392 425	29 911 574	34 686 076	33 270 414	51 445 257	48 267 989	55 545 645	51 672 665
Henan	22 745 054	21 469 540	25 490 705	24 834 806	37 949 774	36 472 799	43 802 724	41 731 476
Shandong	24 311 397	24 565 151	27 920 899	27 598 139	37 736 680	36 682 472	42 913 185	41 478 919
Jiangsu	20 790 461	20 461 731	22 418 473	22 086 135	30 767 523	29 753 590	34 123 252	32 933 560
Guangdong	17 631 534	17 138 525	21 810 060	20 990 789	30 312 111	28 987 509	32 151 260	30 678 481
Hebei	18 298 265	17 686 379	23 381 735	22 306 046	27 125 608	25 879 899	31 210 112	29 872 643
Hunan	17 526 418	15 700 536	19 317 036	17 865 250	28 052 125	25 958 030	31 497 631	29 160 361
Anhui	16 109 956	14 233 681	16 181 927	15 059 730	25 763 836	23 902 111	29 026 412	27 154 593
Hubei	14 331 671	13 458 022	17 306 618	16 402 726	24 547 939	23 260 179	27 828 085	26 142 416
Zhejiang	12 233 408	10 632 339	14 790 590	13 527 983	20 166 996	18 717 597	21 363 128	20 082 887
Liaoning	9 760 372	8 784 775	13 852 340	13 093 860	18 225 145	17 496 549	20 152 574	19 307 120
Jiangxi	8 576 804	8 196 061	10 874 841	10 193 178	17 114 253	16 071 218	19 491 767	18 218 410
Yunnan	8 771 950	8 700 787	10 247 452	10 262 073	16 499 814	16 053 885	18 995 900	17 976 687
Heilongjiang	6 487 678	5 409 631	10 589 553	9 528 718	16 721 245	15 944 267	18 048 747	17 167 185
Shaanxi	8 549 454	7 331 827	10 896 670	9 870 245	14 967 717	13 936 652	17 070 054	15 812 232
Guizhou	7 598 023	7 439 287	8 684 790	8 455 731	14 640 837	13 912 105	16 768 810	15 622 241
Fujian	6 895 547	6 247 174	8 692 706	8 064 517	13 308 562	12 564 355	15 434 048	14 614 227
Shanxi	7 644 677	6 669 808	9 528 116	8 486 951	13 161 639	12 129 811	14 958 318	13 800 528
Jilin	6 012 087	5 277 986	8 172 363	7 496 300	11 554 343	11 005 681	12 624 084	12 035 706
Gansu	6 898 183	6 029 919	6 571 652	6 058 917	10 123 880	9 445 311	11 591 905	10 779 180
Hainan[a]	–	–	–	–	–	–	3 418 860	3 139 216
Qinghai	852 515	824 019	1 137 994	1 007 610	2 004 865	1 890 830	2 310 183	2 146 769
Autonomous regions								
Guangxi	10 102 541	9 458 281	10 671 448	10 173 569	18 851 663	17 569 758	22 156 180	20 088 704
Nei Mongol	3 431 883	2 668 221	6 705 441	5 643 197	10 052 855	9 221 426	11 155 668	10 300 850
Xinjiang Uygur	2 597 769	2 275 839	3 894 740	3 375 327	6 732 231	6 349 307	7 823 195	7 333 688
Ningxia Hui	–	–	1 108 421	999 069	2 006 845	1 888 731	2 389 470	2 265 975
Tibet	–	–	597 296	653 929	921 238	942 385	1 098 912	1 097 117
Others[b]	4 314 461	4 272 425	–	–	–	–	–	–
Municipalities								
Shanghai	3 319 575	2 884 842	5 369 047	5 447 411	5 909 980	5 949 720	6 806 091	6 535 761
Beijing	1 597 868	1 170 281	3 891 140	3 677 355	4 670 631	4 560 032	5 593 461	5 225 953
Tianjin	1 480 280	1 213 551	1 726 882	1 634 773	3 941 913	3 822 224	4 470 746	4 314 681
China	301 262 256	280 112 192	356 517 011	338 064 748	515 277 505	488 636 422	581 820 407	548 690 231

Source: Yao Xinwa and Yin Hua, *Basic Data of China's Population*, Data User Service Series No. 1 (China Population Publishing House).

a/ Hainan was part of Guangdong Province until 1988.

b/ Including the population in two places, Rehe and Xikang, which were not shown in the later censuses.

Table C.3 Percentage female in total population and sex ratios by administrative region: censuses of 1964, 1982 and 1990

Administrative region	1964			1982			1990		
	Percent-age female	Males/ 100 females	Females/ 100 males	Percent-age female	Males/ 100 females	Females/ 100 males	Percent-age female	Males/ 100 females	Females/ 100 males
Provinces									
Sichuan	49.0	104.2	95.9	48.4	106.6	93.8	48.2	107.4	93.0
Henan	49.3	102.6	97.4	49.0	104.0	96.1	48.8	105.0	95.3
Shandong	49.7	101.2	98.8	49.3	102.9	97.2	49.2	103.4	96.7
Jiangsu	49.6	101.5	98.5	49.2	103.4	96.7	49.1	103.6	96.5
Guangdong	49.0	103.9	96.2	48.9	104.6	95.6	48.8	104.8	95.4
Hebei	48.8	104.8	95.4	48.8	104.8	95.4	48.9	104.4	95.7
Hunan	48.0	108.1	92.4	48.1	108.1	92.5	48.1	108.0	92.6
Anhui	48.2	107.4	93.1	48.1	107.8	92.8	48.3	106.9	93.6
Hubei	48.7	105.5	94.8	48.7	105.5	94.8	48.4	106.4	93.9
Zhejiang	47.8	109.3	91.4	48.1	107.7	92.8	48.4	106.4	94.0
Liaoning	48.6	105.8	94.5	49.0	104.2	96.0	48.9	104.4	95.8
Jiangxi	48.4	106.7	93.7	48.4	106.4	93.9	48.3	107.0	93.4
Yunnan	50.0	100.1	99.9	49.3	102.8	97.3	48.6	105.7	94.6
Heilongjiang	47.4	111.1	90.0	48.8	104.9	95.4	48.7	105.1	95.1
Shaanxi	47.5	110.4	90.6	48.2	107.4	93.1	48.1	108.0	92.6
Guizhou	49.3	102.7	97.4	48.7	105.2	95.0	48.2	107.3	93.2
Fujian	48.1	107.8	92.8	48.4	105.9	94.4	48.6	105.6	94.7
Shanxi	47.1	112.3	89.1	48.0	108.5	92.2	48.0	108.4	92.3
Jilin	47.8	109.0	91.7	48.8	105.0	95.3	48.8	104.9	95.3
Gansu	48.0	108.4	92.2	48.3	107.2	93.3	48.2	107.5	93.0
Hainan[a]	–	–	–	–	–	–	47.9	108.9	91.8
Qinghai	47.0	112.9	88.5	48.5	106.0	94.3	48.2	107.6	92.9
Autonomous regions									
Guangxi	48.8	104.9	95.3	48.2	107.3	93.2	47.6	110.3	90.7
Nei Mongol	45.7	118.8	84.2	47.8	109.0	91.7	48.0	108.3	92.3
Xinjiang Uygur	46.4	115.4	86.7	48.5	106.0	94.3	48.4	106.7	93.7
Ningxia Hui	47.4	110.9	90.1	48.4	106.3	94.1	48.7	105.4	94.8
Tibet	52.3	91.3	109.4	50.6	97.8	102.3	50.0	100.2	99.8
Municipalities									
Shanghai	50.4	98.6	101.4	50.2	99.3	100.7	49.0	104.1	96.0
Beijing	48.6	105.8	94.4	49.4	102.4	97.6	48.3	107.0	93.4
Tianjin	48.6	105.6	94.7	49.2	103.1	97.0	49.1	103.6	95.7
China	48.7	105.4	94.8	48.7	105.4	94.8	48.5	106.0	94.3

Source: Yao Xinwa and Yin Hua, *Basic Data of China's Population*, Data User Service Series No. 1 (China Population Publishing House).

[a] Hainan was part of Guangdong Province until 1988.

Table C.4 Number of deaths by age group and sex, and percentage female deaths: 1981 and 1989

Age group	1981				1989			
	Both sexes	Male	Female	Percentage female	Both sexes	Male	Female	Percentage female
0-4	1 003 140	520 791	482 349	48.1	721 060	362 910	358 150	49.7
5-9	136 044	76 721	59 323	43.6	72 296	43 309	28 987	40.1
10-14	93 328	52 285	41 043	44.0	58 472	34 273	24 199	41.4
15-19	117 072	63 478	53 594	45.8	121 952	68 945	53 007	43.6
20-24	107 288	56 690	50 598	47.2	161 052	90 153	70 899	44.0
25-29	133 967	68 520	65 447	48.9	119 438	68 135	51 303	43.0
30-34	117 154	62 470	54 684	46.7	134 937	79 854	55 083	40.8
35-39	119 794	66 728	53 066	44.3	159 588	95 933	63 655	39.9
40-44	155 418	90 181	65 237	42.0	166 239	101 537	64 702	39.0
45-49	224 404	131 782	92 622	41.3	206 922	127 490	79 432	38.4
50-54	306 032	182 430	123 602	40.4	311 840	193 182	118 658	38.1
55-59	411 604	246 363	165 241	40.1	449 615	282 766	166 849	37.1
60-64	551 864	323 519	228 345	41.4	610 494	378 512	231 982	38.0
65-69	659 026	373 044	285 982	43.4	749 605	447 754	301 851	40.3
70-74	750 633	395 112	355 521	47.4	838 255	469 272	368 983	44.0
75-79	672 147	322 944	349 203	52.0	753 162	388 658	364 504	48.4
80-84	452 591	192 310	260 281	57.5	570 799	255 038	315 761	55.3
85+	262 434	90 545	171 889	65.4	367 233	132 051	235 182	64.0
Total	6 273 940	3 315 913	2 958 027	47.1	6 572 959	3 619 772	2 953 187	44.9

Source: Yao Xinwu and Yin Hua, *Basic Data of China's Population*, Data User Service Series No. 1 (China Population Publishing House).

Table C.5 Infant mortality rate by sex, administrative division and urban-rural residence: 1989-1990

(Per thousand live births)

Administrative region	Total			Urban			Rural		
	Both sexes	Male	Female	Both sexes	Male	Female	Both sexes	Male	Female
Provinces									
Sichuan	38.4	36.2	40.8	31.3	32.0	30.6	39.7	37.0	42.7
Henan	18.5	16.2	21.3	12.8	12.0	13.7	19.4	16.8	22.3
Shandong	12.9	11.4	14.7	9.1	8.4	9.8	14.0	12.2	16.1
Jiangsu	15.0	15.0	15.1	11.6	11.6	11.7	15.7	15.6	15.8
Guangdong	15.9	14.7	17.1	13.7	12.0	15.6	16.8	15.9	17.8
Hebei	9.2	9.3	9.1	8.0	8.3	7.8	9.4	9.5	9.4
Hunan	38.1	36.2	40.2	23.0	22.9	23.2	40.4	38.2	42.8
Anhui	26.1	24.7	27.6	18.1	17.9	18.3	27.5	25.9	29.2
Hubei	25.1	25.2	25.0	15.8	16.3	15.2	27.8	27.8	27.8
Zhejiang	17.1	15.7	18.7	12.6	12.0	13.2	19.0	17.2	21.1
Liaoning	18.7	18.9	18.4	17.1	18.1	16.0	20.0	19.5	20.5
Jiangxi	43.0	36.5	50.1	27.6	23.8	31.8	45.7	38.8	53.3
Yunnan	65.8	66.7	64.9	32.2	34.4	29.8	69.7	70.4	69.0
Heilongjiang	18.4	19.9	16.8	13.3	14.4	12.1	22.3	24.0	20.3
Shaanxi	22.0	21.1	23.0	16.7	16.2	17.2	23.0	22.0	24.0
Guizhou	52.4	49.9	55.0	37.9	36.1	39.8	55.3	52.6	57.9
Fujian	23.0	20.1	26.2	19.0	17.9	20.3	23.8	20.6	27.3
Shanxi	19.2	19.2	19.2	14.1	14.1	14.1	20.8	20.8	20.8
Jilin	24.4	25.3	23.5	16.4	17.3	15.4	28.7	29.5	27.8
Gansu	31.5	29.0	34.2	18.4	18.5	18.3	33.9	31.0	37.2
Hainan	29.2	27.3	31.4	21.8	20.1	21.8	31.1	29.2	33.3
Qinghai	66.3	69.6	62.8	25.8	29.2	22.3	75.5	79.0	72.0
Autonomous regions									
Guangxi	44.0	27.3	63.7	22.4	15.0	30.8	46.5	28.7	67.5
Nei Mongol	29.0	27.5	30.6	17.0	17.3	16.7	34.8	32.4	37.4
Xinjiang Uygur	58.5	63.1	53.7	27.3	30.2	24.2	67.7	72.8	62.3
Ningxia Hui	37.3	38.9	35.6	14.2	15.8	12.5	42.3	44.0	40.6
Tibet	96.2	105.0	87.0	38.3	39.6	37.0	101.0	110.4	91.2
Municipalities									
Shanghai	12.4	13.9	10.9	11.2	12.1	10.2	14.9	17.6	12.1
Beijing	8.8	9.5	8.0	9.2	9.7	8.6	8.1	9.1	7.0
Tianjin	10.7	11.3	10.0	12.1	13.6	10.6	8.8	8.6	8.8
China	27.3	25.4	29.4	–	–	–	–	–	–

Source: Huang Rongqing and Liu Yan, *Mortality Data of China Population*, Data User Service Series No. 4 (China Population Publishing House).

Table C.6 Illiteracy and semi-illiteracy rates by administrative division and sex: 1982 and 1990 censuses

Administrative divisions	1982 census			1990 census		
	Both sexes	Male	Female	Both sexes	Male	Female
Provinces						
Sichuan	32.0	19.8	45.0	21.3	13.0	30.1
Henan	37.0	23.4	51.0	23.1	14.1	32.3
Shandong	36.8	21.7	52.1	23.0	13.3	32.9
Jiangsu	34.6	19.3	50.4	22.7	12.1	33.7
Guangdong	22.9	9.2	37.1	15.1	5.8	24.6
Hebei	29.6	17.5	42.1	21.6	12.8	30.7
Hunan	23.9	13.2	35.5	17.0	9.2	25.4
Anhui	46.2	29.6	64.1	34.4	21.2	48.3
Hubei	31.1	17.7	45.2	22.3	12.5	32.7
Zhejiang	31.2	19.1	44.2	23.0	13.3	33.1
Liaoning	16.6	10.0	23.4	11.5	6.6	16.6
Jiangxi	32.1	16.9	48.4	24.1	12.4	36.6
Yunnan	49.3	34.5	64.4	37.4	24.4	51.2
Heilongjiang	22.2	14.4	30.4	14.9	9.4	20.7
Shaanxi	33.2	22.3	44.9	25.1	16.4	34.5
Guizhou	47.9	29.3	67.4	36.7	21.4	53.2
Fujian	37.2	18.3	57.1	23.2	10.6	36.3
Shanxi	24.4	16.0	33.5	15.8	10.1	22.0
Jilin	21.8	15.0	28.9	14.3	9.4	19.3
Gansu	48.1	32.7	64.7	39.2	26.3	53.1
Hainan	–	–	–	21.2	9.9	33.2
Qinghai	46.8	31.9	62.8	40.0	26.9	54.4
Autonomous regions						
Guangxi	25.0	12.3	38.6	16.3	7.5	25.7
Nei Mongol	31.1	21.7	41.5	21.7	14.4	29.6
Xinjiang Uygur	30.7	25.4	36.4	19.5	15.8	23.6
Ningxia Hui	43.0	29.5	57.6	33.4	22.4	45.1
Tibet	73.2	61.5	84.3	69.3	55.4	83.1
Municipalities						
Shanghai	16.7	7.4	25.9	13.5	6.0	21.4
Beijing	15.0	7.8	22.3	10.9	5.4	16.9
Tianjin	17.2	8.4	26.3	11.6	5.3	18.0
China	31.9	19.2	45.2	22.2	13.0	31.9

Source: Yao Xinwu and Yin Hua, *Basic Data of China's Population*, Data User Service Series No. 1 (China Population Publishing House).

Note: The illiteracy and semi-illiteracy rates are percentages of illiterate and semi-illiterate persons among persons aged 12 years and over at the 1982 census and 15 years and over at the 1990 census.

Table D.1 Average family/household size by administrative division: 1982 and 1990 censuses

Administrative division	Average family size	
	1982	1990
Provinces		
Sichuan	4.25	3.66
Henan	4.73	4.22
Shandong	4.16	3.75
Jiangsu	3.91	3.66
Guangdong	4.80	4.42
Hebei	4.14	3.89
Hunan	4.21	3.77
Anhui	4.64	4.14
Hubei	4.53	4.01
Zhejiang	3.96	3.46
Liaoning	4.09	3.59
Jiangxi	4.94	4.40
Yunnan	5.17	4.51
Heilongjiang	4.50	3.90
Shaanxi	4.48	4.07
Guizhou	4.93	4.41
Fujian	4.85	4.43
Shanxi	4.07	3.88
Jilin	4.39	3.86
Gansu	5.07	4.55
Hainan	–	4.57
Qinghai	5.16	4.64
Autonomous regions		
Guangxi	5.14	4.65
Nei Mongol	4.51	4.00
Xinjiang Uygur	4.33	4.39
Ningxia Hui	5.09	4.57
Tibet	5.06	5.20
Municipalities		
Shanghai	3.60	3.10
Beijing	3.69	3.20
Tianjin	3.90	3.34
China	4.43	3.97

Source: Yao Xinwu and Yin Hua, *Basic Data of China's Population*, Data User Service Series No. 1 (China Population Publishing House).

Table D.2 Percentage distribution of households by household size and administrative region: 1992

Administrative region	Household size (number of persons)								Total
	1	2	3	4	5	6	7	8 and over	
Provinces									
Sichuan	7.8	12.0	30.4	25.7	13.1	6.2	2.6	2.2	100.0
Henan	4.9	10.1	21.3	29.3	19.4	8.6	4.1	2.3	100.0
Shandong	5.8	12.5	29.8	29.4	14.3	5.5	1.7	0.9	100.0
Jiangsu	6.4	11.8	29.4	26.6	16.1	6.4	2.1	1.2	100.0
Guangdong	8.2	8.4	11.4	21.3	21.1	13.4	7.4	8.8	100.0
Hebei	6.8	12.8	25.6	28.5	15.1	6.9	2.6	1.7	100.0
Hunan	6.7	12.9	24.1	31.2	15.9	6.0	2.0	1.2	100.0
Anhui	6.4	10.0	21.3	29.0	18.5	9.0	3.7	2.1	100.0
Hubei	4.3	10.2	23.9	31.0	18.7	7.3	2.9	1.7	100.0
Zhejiang	10.1	14.2	31.2	26.4	11.8	4.2	1.4	0.7	100.0
Liaoning	4.0	13.0	38.5	25.9	11.7	4.5	1.3	1.0	100.0
Jiangxi	3.8	7.7	18.5	28.4	21.7	10.6	4.8	4.3	100.0
Yunnan	4.5	8.3	17.9	28.3	19.8	11.0	5.5	4.6	100.0
Heilongjiang	3.2	10.9	36.1	27.5	13.9	5.8	1.8	0.8	100.0
Shaanxi	5.6	11.2	21.4	27.8	19.1	9.0	4.0	1.9	100.0
Guizhou	4.9	8.4	18.0	24.8	22.7	11.9	5.6	3.7	100.0
Fujian	5.1	7.0	14.9	25.5	23.3	12.2	6.1	5.8	100.0
Shanxi	6.6	11.9	25.1	28.6	17.1	6.8	2.6	1.3	100.0
Jilin	3.7	11.8	35.2	27.7	13.5	4.8	1.9	1.4	100.0
Gansu	3.1	6.2	19.4	26.8	19.5	11.7	6.6	6.7	100.0
Hainan	6.6	8.9	15.6	19.1	19.8	12.8	8.2	9.0	100.0
Qinghai	3.4	6.4	15.0	24.0	21.9	12.4	7.6	9.3	100.0
Autonomous regions									
Guangxi	5.2	7.5	13.4	21.8	22.1	13.1	8.6	8.3	100.0
Nei Mongol	4.3	9.6	24.8	30.5	19.3	6.8	2.7	1.9	100.0
Xinjiang Uygur	4.7	9.8	18.0	21.3	17.9	11.7	7.6	8.9	100.0
Ningxia Hui	2.7	7.5	18.4	26.0	21.3	12.3	6.4	5.4	100.0
Tibet	6.4	10.5	14.7	20.6	12.8	11.7	8.6	14.7	100.0
Municipalities									
Shanghai	11.6	21.6	38.3	17.1	8.0	2.3	0.7	0.3	100.0
Beijing	7.8	15.7	40.2	20.9	9.5	3.5	1.3	0.9	100.0
Tianjin	6.3	14.3	41.1	22.0	10.4	3.7	1.3	0.9	100.0
China	5.9	11.2	26.2	25.8	16.4	7.8	3.6	3.1	100.0

Source: State Statistical Burean, *1994 Statistical Yearbook of China*, tables 3-15.

Table D.3 Total fertility rates in 28 provinces, autonomous regions and municipalities: selected years, 1973-1987

Administrative division[a/]	1973	1975	1977	1978	1979	1981	1983	1985	1987
Provinces									
Sichuan	5.46	4.44	2.50	1.88	1.94	2.35	2.07	1.94	2.26
Henan	4.97	3.54	2.99	3.16	3.14	2.72	2.60	2.11	3.06
Shandong	3.73	3.04	2.34	2.13	2.43	2.20	2.09	1.91	2.68
Jiangsu	2.70	2.22	1.99	1.90	1.86	2.02	1.73	1.58	2.04
Guangdong	4.84	3.84	3.34	3.61	3.77	3.17	2.98	2.56	2.76
Hebei	3.84	2.57	2.28	2.35	2.27	2.73	2.47	2.36	2.81
Hunan	4.56	3.97	2.71	2.46	2.52	2.91	2.86	2.36	2.73
Anhui	4.86	3.64	3.00	3.34	3.40	3.16	2.76	2.41	2.69
Hubei	4.02	3.24	2.71	2.53	2.93	2.38	2.52	2.50	2.97
Zhejiang	3.27	2.67	2.36	2.18	2.28	1.94	1.88	1.40	1.69
Liaoning	3.41	2.14	1.88	2.24	2.09	1.82	1.50	1.34	1.88
Jiangxi	6.78	5.83	5.26	4.77	4.03	2.75	2.93	2.61	2.90
Yunnan	5.52	5.32	4.99	4.54	3.99	3.86	3.44	3.04	3.20
Heilongjiang	4.95	3.26	2.46	2.11	2.81	2.11	1.85	1.62	1.94
Shaanxi	4.44	3.29	2.62	2.69	2.87	2.32	2.47	2.64	2.97
Guizhou	6.66	6.32	4.68	3.84	4.12	4.25	3.55	3.32	3.69
Fujian	5.34	4.22	4.04	3.49	2.86	2.83	2.96	2.44	2.35
Shanxi	4.66	3.42	2.70	2.28	2.23	2.37	2.39	2.40	2.46
Jilin	4.19	2.50	2.33	2.46	2.70	1.85	1.62	1.52	1.83
Gansu	5.80	3.49	2.79	3.09	3.49	2.75	2.63	2.55	2.61
Qinghai	5.87	4.94	5.11	4.87	5.00	3.97	3.04	2.52	2.72
Autonomous regions									
Guangxi	5.66	5.11	3.99	3.65	3.98	4.04	3.55	3.68	3.59
Nei Mongol	4.26	3.04	2.70	2.55	2.47	2.72	2.33	2.01	2.22
Xinjiang Uygur	5.49	4.93	4.27	4.05	3.79	4.18	4.07	3.66	3.75
Ningxia Hui	5.84	6.19	4.13	4.35	4.79	3.95	3.16	2.77	3.12
Municipalities									
Shanghai	1.54	1.12	1.15	1.20	1.20	1.28	1.23	1.00	1.48
Beijing	2.60	1.40	1.48	1.37	1.46	1.58	1.47	1.32	1.58
Tianjin	2.30	2.00	1.72	1.66	1.54	1.74	1.68	1.51	1.69
China	4.53	3.58	2.84	2.73	2.75	2.61	2.42	2.20	2.59

Source: 1982 One-per-Thousand Fertility Sampling Survey, and 1988 Two-per-Thousand Fertility and Birth Control Sampling Survey, reported in Li Bohua, "Levels, trends and determinants of fertility in China: 1973-1987", *Asia-Pacific Population Journal*, vol. 5, No. 2, 1990.

[a/] At the time of the 1982 Survey, what is currently Hainan Province was part of Guangdong Province. This survey also did not include Tibet. Since comparable data are not available, those two provinces are excluded from this table.

Table D.4 Percentage of currently married women using contraception by method, total fertility rate, socio-economic development index and cluster ranking: 29 administrative divisions of China: 1988

Administrative division	Contraceptive method (%)				Total fertility rate	Socio-economic index (SES)	SES rank	Percentage ethnic minority population
	Sterili-zation	IUD	Others	All methods				
Provinces								
Sichuan	33.3	62.0	4.7	100.0	1.65	6.9	3	3.7
Henan	54.7	41.7	3.6	100.0	2.66	10.9	3	1.1
Shandong	59.4	34.9	5.8	100.0	2.30	17.1	2	0.5
Jiangsu	56.4	36.7	6.9	100.0	1.77	18.0	1	0.2
Guangdong	60.6	35.3	4.1	100.0	2.64	18.9	1	1.8
Hebei	61.9	31.7	6.4	100.0	2.36	17.4	2	1.6
Hunan	54.1	37.0	8.9	100.0	2.44	11.7	2	4.1
Anhui	54.5	33.3	12.2	100.0	2.48	11.6	2	0.5
Hubei	56.6	34.1	9.3	100.0	2.66	15.6	2	3.7
Zhejiang	62.3	26.9	10.8	100.0	1.78	17.0	2	0.4
Liaoning	29.2	50.4	20.4	100.0	1.67	24.6	1	8.1
Jiangxi	60.3	30.8	8.9	100.0	2.79	9.9	3	0.1
Yunnan	17.4	60.8	21.8	100.0	2.84	3.9	3	31.7
Heilongjiang	39.3	52.5	8.2	100.0	1.82	19.4	1	4.9
Shaanxi	32.6	63.7	3.7	100.0	2.65	10.0	3	0.5
Guizhou	33.3	60.8	5.9	100.0	3.33	4.3	3	26.0
Fujian	63.2	26.7	10.1	100.0	2.82	13.9	2	1.0
Shanxi	43.1	50.4	6.5	100.0	2.36	18.0	1	0.3
Jilin	34.3	58.6	7.1	100.0	1.66	22.9	1	8.1
Gansu	56.5	35.8	7.7	100.0	2.48	6.6	3	8.0
Hainan	59.3	36.4	4.3	100.0	2.93	n.a.	n.a.	n.a.
Qinghai	31.2	31.9	36.9	100.0	2.71	4.0	3	39.4
Autonomous regions								
Guangxi	11.2	74.7	14.1	100.0	3.16	11.6	2	38.3
Nei Mongol	47.2	38.1	14.7	100.0	2.23	14.3	2	15.5
Xinjiang Uygur	21.2	36.2	42.6	100.0	3.75	12.1	2	59.6
Ningxia Hui	19.7	37.4	42.9	100.0	3.16	8.4	3	31.9
Municipalities								
Shanghai	29.3	37.8	32.9	100.0	1.02	26.1	1	0.4
Beijing	24.5	49.4	26.1	100.0	1.28	27.0	1	3.5
Tianjin	32.2	45.3	22.5	100.0	1.39	24.1	1	2.1

Source: Quanhe Yang, "Provincial patterns of contraceptive use in China", *Asia-Pacific Population Journal*, vol. 9, No. 4, 1994.

Notes: SES 1 = high development; SES 2 = medium development; SES 3 = low development.
n.a. = not available.

Table D.5 Percentage composition of birth orders by administrative division: 1981 and 1989

Administrative division	1981			1989		
	First	Second	Third and higher	First	Second	Third and higher
Provinces						
Sichuan	56.4	24.1	19.5	60.8	29.3	9.9
Henan	44.4	27.8	27.8	42.7	34.7	22.6
Shandong	60.4	24.7	14.9	48.9	34.1	17.0
Jiangsu	61.4	25.7	12.9	62.0	27.0	11.0
Guangdong	37.0	28.0	35.0	40.7	30.3	29.0
Hebei	52.2	27.5	20.3	47.0	36.1	16.9
Hunan	43.2	30.9	25.9	45.5	35.0	19.5
Anhui	37.4	28.2	34.4	48.7	32.4	18.9
Hubei	50.1	27.8	22.1	45.0	35.5	19.5
Zhejiang	54.1	26.6	19.3	72.1	23.2	4.7
Liaoning	71.6	19.0	9.4	73.6	22.3	4.1
Jiangxi	36.2	28.4	35.4	43.5	32.1	24.4
Yunnan	28.3	22.2	49.5	43.8	32.8	23.4
Heilongjiang	53.9	26.6	19.5	63.2	27.5	9.3
Shaanxi	49.9	26.1	24.0	41.7	32.9	25.4
Guizhou	23.8	20.3	55.9	40.4	26.2	33.4
Fujian	40.9	29.8	29.3	46.2	32.2	21.6
Shanxi	47.8	27.6	24.6	44.6	34.3	21.1
Jilin	60.0	25.3	14.7	60.8	29.1	10.1
Gansu	43.3	25.0	31.7	43.8	33.2	23.0
Hainan	–	–	–	39.1	28.3	32.6
Qinghai	26.8	19.5	53.7	44.9	27.5	27.6
Autonomous regions						
Guangxi	31.2	23.8	45.0	39.6	33.6	26.8
Nei Mongol	44.1	26.6	29.3	52.9	32.4	14.7
Xinjiang Uygur	26.9	18.1	55.0	34.0	20.9	45.1
Ningxia Hui	30.9	20.5	48.6	40.1	30.0	29.9
Tibet	–	–	–	25.0	20.3	54.7
Municipalities						
Shanghai	87.0	12.1	0.9	92.1	7.3	0.6
Beijing	84.1	12.8	3.1	71.7	24.4	3.9
Tianjin	78.5	16.1	5.4	72.4	22.5	5.1
China	47.3	25.6	27.1	49.4	31.3	19.3

Source: Estimates based on 100 per cent tabulation of 1982 and 1990 population census data.

Table D.6 Female mean age at first marriage and mean age at first birth by administrative division: 1981 and 1989

(Years)

Administrative division	1981			1989		
	MAFM	MAFB	Difference	MAFM	MAFB	Difference
Provinces						
Sichuan	21.72	25.49	3.77	21.58	22.66	1.08
Henan	22.71	26.04	3.33	22.12	23.44	1.32
Shandong	23.03	26.21	3.18	22.61	23.70	1.09
Jiangsu	22.69	25.64	2.95	22.07	23.21	1.14
Guangdong	23.10	25.22	2.21	23.42	23.93	0.51
Hebei	22.40	25.88	3.48	21.80	23.35	1.45
Hunan	21.65	24.50	2.85	21.63	22.57	0.94
Anhui	22.45	25.09	2.64	22.08	22.91	0.83
Hubei	22.66	25.15	2.49	21.92	22.93	1.01
Zhejiang	22.28	24.74	2.46	22.54	23.58	1.04
Liaoning	22.98	26.05	3.07	22.34	23.93	1.59
Jiangxi	21.33	23.51	2.18	21.39	22.26	1.57
Yunnan	21.54	24.05	2.51	21.60	22.60	1.00
Heilongjiang	22.12	24.97	2.85	21.87	23.25	1.38
Shaanxi	22.18	24.98	2.80	21.65	23.11	1.46
Guizhou	21.92	24.63	2.71	21.98	22.93	0.95
Fujian	21.34	23.76	2.42	21.36	22.41	1.05
Shanxi	21.47	24.31	2.84	21.66	23.12	1.46
Jilin	22.47	25.44	2.97	21.81	23.12	1.31
Gansu	21.09	23.76	2.67	21.45	22.53	1.08
Hainan	–	–	–	22.67	23.25	0.58
Qinghai	20.81	22.71	1.09	21.68	22.58	0.09
Autonomous regions						
Guangxi	22.59	25.39	2.80	22.58	23.38	0.80
Nei Mongol	21.97	24.53	2.56	22.03	23.24	1.21
Xinjiang Uygur	20.97	24.00	3.03	21.73	22.85	1.12
Ningxia Hui	21.24	23.72	2.48	21.61	22.56	0.95
Tibet	–	–	–	23.06	23.66	0.60
Municipalities						
Shanghai	25.64	27.13	1.49	23.60	26.20	2.60
Beijing	24.65	27.41	2.76	23.77	25.66	1.89
Tianjin	24.62	27.59	2.97	22.96	25.02	2.06
China	22.43	25.36	2.93	22.06	23.20	1.14

Source: Estimates derived from 100 per cent tabulation of the data from the 1982 and 1990 censuses.

MAFM – mean age at first marriage.
MAFB – mean age at first birth.

Table E.1 Distribution of employed persons by administrative division and sex: 1990 census

Administrative division	Employed persons (thousands)			Sex composition (%)	
	Both sexes	Male	Female	Male	Female
Provinces					
Sichuan	68 544	36 481	32 063	53.2	46.8
Henan	50 191	26 897	23 294	53.6	46.4
Shandong	50 772	27 018	23 754	53.2	46.8
Jiangsu	41 868	22 076	19 792	52.7	47.3
Guangdong	33 657	18 384	15 273	54.6	45.4
Hebei	34 101	19 149	14 952	56.2	43.8
Hunan	34 897	19 323	15 574	55.4	44.6
Anhui	33 466	18 088	15 378	54.0	46.0
Hubei	31 569	17 105	14 464	54.2	45.8
Zhejiang	24 575	14 360	10 215	58.4	41.6
Liaoning	22 381	12 782	9 599	57.1	42.9
Jiangxi	20 455	11 265	9 180	55.1	44.9
Yunnan	21 048	11 063	9 985	52.6	47.4
Heilongjiang	17 450	10 698	6 752	61.3	38.7
Shaanxi	18 101	10 221	7 880	56.5	43.5
Guizhou	18 012	9 517	8 495	52.8	47.2
Fujian	14 955	8 915	6 040	59.6	40.4
Shanxi	14 952	9 123	5 829	61.0	39.0
Jilin	12 865	7 644	5 221	59.4	40.6
Gansu	13 174	7 097	6 077	53.9	46.1
Hainan	3 335	1 801	1 534	54.0	46.0
Qinghai	2 413	1 338	1 075	55.4	44.6
Autonomous regions					
Guangxi	22 926	12 323	10 603	53.8	46.2
Nei Mongol	11 192	6 638	4 554	59.3	40.7
Xinjiang Uygur	7 557	4 239	3 317	56.1	43.9
Ningxia Hui	2 409	1 292	1 117	53.6	46.4
Tibet	1 109	613	496	55.3	44.7
Municipalities					
Shanghai	8 059	4 380	3 679	54.3	45.7
Beijing	6 226	3 564	2 662	57.2	42.8
Tianjin	4 995	2 836	2 159	56.8	43.2
China	647 244	356 230	291 013	55.0	45.0

Source: Estimates derived from 100 per cent tabulation of the data from the 1982 and 1990 censuses.

REFERENCES

Abou Zahr, Carla and Erica Royston, *Maternal Mortality: A Global Fact Book* (Geneva, World Health Organization, 1991).

Arnold, Fred and Liu Zhaoxiang, "Sex preference, fertility and family planning in China", *Population and Development Review*, vol. 12, No. 2, 1986.

Caldwell, John and others, "Population trends in China: a perspective provided by the 1982 census", in Li Chengrui and others, eds., *A Census of One Billion People*, papers for the International Seminar on China's 1982 Population Census, 26-31 March 1984, Beijing.

Centre for Reproductive Law and Policy, *Women of the World: Formal Laws and Policies Affecting Their Reproductive Lives* (New York, August 1995).

Cheng, C.Z., "The fertility decline in China: the contributions of changes in marital status and marital fertility", *Asia-Pacific Population Journal*, vol. 8, No. 2, 1993.

China Population Association, *The Population Situation in China: The Insiders' View* (State Family Planning Commission of China, October 1996).

China Population Information and Research Centre, "Population and development in China", *China Population Today*, vol. 11, No. 3, 1994, Special Issue for the International Conference on Population and Development, Cairo, 1994.

———, *China Population Today*, vol. 12, Nos. 3-4, 1995.

Coale, Ansley J. and Judith Banister, "Five decades of missing females in China", *Demography*, vol. 31, No. 3, 1994.

Conly, Shanti R. and Sharon L. Camp, *China's Family Planning Program: Challenging the Myths*, Country Study Series No. 1 (Washington D.C., The Population Crisis Committee, 1992).

Davin, Delia, *Woman Work: Women and Party in Revolutionary China* (Oxford, Clarendon Press, 1976).

———, "Women in the countryside of China", in Margery Wolf and Roxana Witka, eds., *Women in Chinese Society* (Stanford, California, Stanford University Press, 1975).

Economist Intelligence Unit, *China: Country Profile, 1994-95.*

Europa Publishers Ltd., *The Far East and Australasia 1995*, 26th edition.

Government of China, *Second Report of the People's Republic of China on the Implementation of the Nairobi Forward-looking Strategies for the Advancement of Women* (Beijing, February 1994).

Gu, Baochang and Liu Peihang, "A review of study of Chinese women", *China Population Today*, vol. 10, No. 3, 1993.

Gu, Baochang and Krishna Roy, "Sex ratio at birth in China, with reference to other areas in East Asia: what we know", *Asia-Pacific Population Journal*, vol. 10, No. 3, 1995.

Huang Rongqing and Liu Yan, *Mortality Data of Chinese Population*, Data Users Service Series No. 4 (China Population Publishing House).

Information Office of the State Council, *The Situation of Chinese Women* (Beijing, June 1994).

Jamison, Dean T. and others, *China: The Health Sector,* a World Bank Country Study.

Jiang Zhenghua and Zeng Yi, "Family size, structure and child development", in *Family Planning, Health and Family Well Being,* Proceedings of the United Nations Expert Group Meeting on Family Planning, Health and Family Well Being, Bangalore, India, 26-30 October 1992 (New York, 1996) (ST/ESA/SER.R/131).

Li, Bohua, "Levels, trends and determinants of fertility in China: 1973-1987", *Asia-Pacific Population Journal,* vol. 5, No. 2, 1990.

Li Rose Maria and Susan F. Newcomer, "The exclusion of never-married women from Chinese fertility surveys", *Studies in Family Planning,* vol. 27, No.3, May/June 1996.

Mackeras, Colin and Amanda Yorke, *The Cambridge Handbook of Contemporary China* (Cambridge University Press, 1991).

Ma Xia, "An analysis of the size of domestic household and the family in China", in Li Chengrui and others, eds., *A Census of One Billion People,* papers for the International Seminar on China's 1982 Population Census, 26-31 March 1984 (Beijing, April 1984).

Peng Peiyun, "The population of China: problems and strategy", *China Population Today,* vol. 9, No. 4, 1992.

Rosen, Stanley, "Women and political participation in China", *Pacific Affairs,* vol. 68, No. 3, 1995.

Selvaratnam, S., "Population and status of women", *Asia-Pacific Population Journal,* vol. 3, No. 2, 1988.

State Family Planning Commission of China, *Population Problem and Family Planning in China,* October 1993.

State Statistical Bureau, *1994 Statistical Yearbook of China; 1995 Statistical Yearbook of China; Sample Survey on the Situation of Chinese Children,* July 1992; and *Preliminary Results of National Child Survey, 1994.*

Sun Jingxin, "The employed population in China as compared with other countries", in Li Chengrui and others, eds, *A Census of Billion People,* papers for the International Seminar on China's 1982 Population Census, 26-31 March 1984 (Beijing, April 1984).

Tu Ping and Peng Xizha, "China's population: status and challenges", *China Population Today,* vol. 11, No. 5, 1994.

United Nations, *Case Studies in Population Policy: China,* Population Policy Paper No. 20 (Department of International Economic and Social Affairs, New York, 1989).

————, *World Population Prospects: The 1994 Revision* (Department for Economic and Social Information and Policy Analysis, New York, 1995) (ST/ESA/SER.A/145).

United Nations Economic and Social Commission for Asia and the Pacific, *Human Resources Development: Effectiveness of Programme Delivery at the Local Level in Countries of the ESCAP Region,* Development Papers No. 16, 1994.

————, *Women in Politics in Asia and the Pacific,* Proceedings of the Seminar on the Participation of Women in Politics as an Aspect of Human Resources Development, 18-20 November 1992, Seoul.

United Nations Children's Fund, "An analysis of the situation of children and women in China" (draft) (Beijing, August 1992).

Wang Peng and Yang Quanhe, "Age at marriage and first birth interval: the emerging change in sexual behaviour among young couples in China", *Population and Development Review,* vol. 22, No. 2, 1996.

Wei Zhangling, *Status of Women: China,* UNESCO Principal Regional Office for Asia and the Pacific, 1989.

Worden, Robert L., Andrea Matles Saveda and Ronald E. Dolan, *China: A Country Study,* 4th edition, Federal Research Division, Library of Congress, Washington D.C., 1988.

World Bank, *China: Comprehensive Maternal and Child Health Programme: Staff Appraisal Report* (Report No. 13025-CHA), September 1994.

Yao Xinwu and Yin Hua, *Basic Data of China's Population,* Data User Service Series No. 1 (China Population Publishing House).

Zheng, Y. and others, Causes and implications of the recent increase in the reported sex ratio at birth in China", *Population and Development Review,* vol. 19, No. 2, 1993.